SIU

SIU

SPECIAL INVESTIGATIONS UNIT

JACK MORGAN

TATE PUBLISHING
AND ENTERPRISES, LLC

Published by Tate Publishing & Enterprises, LLC
127 E. Trade Center Terrace | Mustang, Oklahoma 73064 USA
1.888.361.9473 | www.tatepublishing.com

Tate Publishing is committed to excellence in the publishing industry. The company reflects the philosophy established by the founders, based on Psalm 68:11,
"The Lord gave the word and great was the company of those who published it."

Book design copyright © 2012 by Tate Publishing, LLC. All rights reserved.
Cover design by Joel Uber
Interior design by Cheryl Moore

Published in the United States of America

ISBN: 978-1-61862-084-2
1. True Crime / General
2. Biography & Autobiography / General
12.04.12

For my beautiful wife, Barb. Thank you for being
by my side through all this and more.

TABLE OF CONTENTS

FOREWORD

Very few people understand the impact insurance fraud has on American consumers and our economy. The impact is tremendous, costing billions of dollars in fraudulent claims and ultimately higher insurance premiums for American consumers.

My friend Jack Morgan not only understands the seriousness of insurance fraud but has spent a career battling against it. In the pages that follow, you will find but a brief summary of many of the fascinating claims and lawsuits spanning his career in the field of insurance special investigations.

For the past several years, I have traveled around the country with Jack, speaking to insurance professionals, attorneys, state fire marshals, law enforcement officials, and firefighters regarding the impact of insurance fraud and how to more effectively investigate questionable insurance claims. I have watched as audiences across the country have sat spellbound hearing the stories of Jack's career that are retold in these pages. More importantly, however, following these seminars, Jack is frequently contacted by those especially in the law enforcement community, thanking him for opening their eyes to crimes that were taking place in their communities, of which they were not even aware. Many of these have resulted in successful criminal prosecutions and saved untold thousands, if not millions, of dollars.

On the pages that follow, you will be introduced to stories that you may even find hard to believe are true. I have said to clients of my law firm for many years, "If we tried to make up these claims, we could never create anything more bizarre than what reality has presented."

Enjoy this book, laugh at some of the stories, and shake your head in disbelief at others. Take away from this book, however, a greater appreciation and understanding for the seriousness of insurance fraud, its impact on our country, and give thanks we are blessed to have people like Jack Morgan who are leading the battle.

—Matthew J. Smith, Esq.

FOREWORD

For the past thirty-five years, I have been involved with the investigation and litigation of insurance-fraud cases. For more than twenty-five of those years I have known and respected Jack Morgan as one of the best in the business. For all who read this fascinating book, I am here to tell you that Jack Morgan has "told it like it is," just as anyone who knows Jack would expect him to do.

Jack Morgan is an icon in this business. He is one of the most well-known and well-respected individuals ever to investigate an insurance-fraud case. When he is on a case, you know that in the end, the truth will come out. I have had the privilege of working with Jack on a number of cases, and in every one of them, the truth did come out. His tenacity is legendary; his expertise is unquestioned. As the stories here show, the search for the truth sometimes takes a strange path. The work is always challenging and often even dangerous. But through it all, it requires a relentless and unwavering commitment to discovering the evidence and finding the truth to prove a case. With the stories told in this book, the reader can see firsthand what it takes to do that, through the experiences and adventures of one who has truly seen it all.

Jack Morgan has given us an insight into the process of investigating insurance fraud known only to those who have taken on that challenge. With clarity and candor, he has shown us what it takes to do the job and do it right. This is a story that needs to be told, and Jack has told it well.

—Guy E. "Sandy" Burnette, Jr., Esq.

PREFACE

My name is Jack Morgan. I am an insurance-fraud investigator in the Special Investigations Unit of a mid-sized insurance company many of you would immediately recognize by the name. It is my job to lead the investigation into questionable claims with suspicious circumstances to determine if the claim is a fraud or if those circumstances are just a coincidence. I seek the truth, whatever it may be. That has been my life's work for the past thirty years.

I was previously with the Ohio State Highway Patrol for ten years. I investigated automobile accidents, fatalities/homicides, and vehicle thefts. I left with the rank of Sergeant. I was in the United States Marine Corps for four years and attained the rank of Staff Sergeant. I spent a tour of duty in Vietnam in a Marine Combat Infantry Company, where I was twice wounded and was awarded two Purple Hearts. I want to recognize and acknowledge my comrades in Golf Company, Second Battalion Seventh Marines, who remain my brothers-in-arms. I remember and honor my friends and brothers who did not make it out of the jungle that day in September of 1966. They made the ultimate sacrifice for their brothers and their country. Every year on that date I remember you all with a shot of Grand Marnier and a toast "to all who did not make it back," as I will do every year to honor your memory.

In recent years, I have been a frequent speaker at training conferences around the country, where I have shared my experiences in the investigation of insurance-fraud cases. I have frequently been asked if I have written a book about my experiences or planned to do so, with an expression of interest should I ever put these experiences to words. With their encouragement, I have finally decided to do just that.

This book includes a collection of some of the most interesting—and sometimes bizarre—cases I have handled. I am blessed to do a job I truly love and which has proven to be both interesting and challenging along the way. I took this job when the opportunity came along at a time when I was trying to support a family of four on a salary of $16,000 after ten years on the job with the State Highway Patrol. It represented a chance for advancement and financial security for my family, which I quickly accepted. I have never looked back.

My job includes both internal and external investigations for my company. Whenever there is a suspicion of fraud or criminal conduct, I am called to investigate the case. I have worked several thousand cases in my years, and they have included almost every kind of situation you can imagine. I have been successful in proving fraud in many of those cases. A lot of people have gone to prison as the result of my work. Just as importantly, a lot of people who were suspected of fraud and criminal conduct were proved to be innocent, and I am proud of those efforts. In the end, it is all about finding the truth, and that is always my first priority.

I have investigated every kind of insurance claim, including staged burglaries, fake death claims, arson cases, jewelry thefts, auto thefts, staged accidents, slip-and-fall claims, disability claims, worker's compensation claims, fraudulent liability claims, and organized fraud rings. I have handled internal investigations involving dishonest agents stealing insurance premiums, adjusters taking kickbacks from contractors or body shops, adjusters directly participating in fraudulent claims, internal theft, and every other kind of misconduct you can imagine. Whenever a problem arises, the SIU is sent to check it out. My work does not end with the investigation of the case; it goes to the very end. I have testified in civil and criminal trials more times than I can count. In my job, once you take on a case you go the distance.

Now sixty-four years old, I know I am nearing the end of my career. In recent years, I have tried to become a mentor to the younger investigators who will soon take my place. I hope to teach them what to do, how to do it properly, and how to find the truth.

Much of my work involves interviewing people. I interview claimants, victims, witnesses, law enforcement officials, and fire-service representatives on an almost daily basis. It is perhaps the most interesting part of my work. Witnesses and the evidence they provide lead us to the truth. With every person I interview, I must determine if their information is accurate, reliable, and truthful. Some witnesses are simply mistaken. Others are untruthful, and the reasons people will lie can include almost anything. The people who will tell those lies include everybody you would expect and then some you might not. I have come across liars who were leading members of their community, clergy, politicians, lawyers, and law enforcement officials. I learned long ago that you can take nothing for granted when interviewing a witness. Who they are and what they are means nothing.

The work of a Special Investigations Unit investigator is not easy. It is a high-stakes game by any measure. Your company wants you to solve the case and do it quickly. They want it done cost effectively too. The work of investigating insurance claims can be costly, and this is always a factor. Time is our enemy, as we have deadlines to meet under the contractual provisions of the insurance policy and the laws of the jurisdiction. State insurance departments require companies to thoroughly investigate claims in making a coverage decision, but they impose additional deadlines on completing the investigation. Failing to do so can result in administrative action and fines against the insurance company just for failing to timely complete an investigation. Insured's and claimants demand a quick decision on their claims, and the lawyers they hire raise the threat of a lawsuit from the very outset of an investigation. The statutes and laws on the investigation of an insurance claim can provide severe penalties for the improper or inadequate investigation of a claim. With the threat of "bad faith" lawsuits seeking millions of dollars in damages, it is a high-stakes game, indeed. In the process of conducting an investigation, we have to do it by the book. Falsely accusing somebody of insurance fraud or arson is a serious accusation with serious implications. In conducting the investigation, we have to follow every law on the books. You cannot violate the privacy rights of an individual in conducting an investigation. If you make a comment that you think somebody has committed a fraud, you will be sued for slander. If you work too closely with law enforcement in conducting an investigation, you can be sued for malicious prosecution. And if you decide to deny a claim and you are wrong, it is not just that you then have to pay the claim. You could end up paying millions in "bad faith" damages to a person wrongfully accused. We are in a business where you just can't afford to make a mistake.

Much of our work involves interacting with public officials and law enforcement. In most states, you are required by law to cooperate with them when they make a request for your investigative file. But if you take too active a part in the investigation, you can be accused of acting on behalf of the law enforcement officials and can jeopardize not only your investigation, but their own investigation. We have to draw a line between cooperating as required by law and crossing that line to become a part of the prosecution team. Even expressing an opinion about a suspect's guilt or innocence can lead to problems. The greatest danger is in jumping to conclusions while conducting an investigation. No matter which way the evidence is lining up, we have to wait until the very end of the investigation to make a decision. If they ask us to do things for them beyond providing our investigative file, we have to draw the line. We cannot act on their behalf to facilitate their investigation other than within the strict limits of the law.

You learn early on in this business that many people do not like insurance companies. Most of the people who have ever had a claim of their own have been unhappy with how it was handled, how quickly it was resolved, or what they were ultimately paid. These are the same people who sit on our juries making decisions about a claim. Selecting a jury can be the most important part of a case, to make sure that the insurance company gets a fair trial. In many cases, an insurance company will conduct a mock trial or jury survey to find out how the members of the community feel about insurance companies in general and about the facts of a particular case. National surveys have been done about the public's perception of insurance companies and the handling of insurance claims. Those surveys have shown that a significant number of people feel there is nothing wrong with trying to get a little something extra from an insurance company when presenting a claim. Some people feel there is nothing wrong with a person setting fire to their own home to collect insurance money. Most people on a jury want to see an insured or claimant recover from their insurance company, and if you have not conducted a thorough investigation to uncover the truth, you will lose every time.

Dealing with the attorneys who represent those insured's and claimants can be a challenge in itself. Some of the high-profile cases we have all seen on television recently have shown that a clever lawyer can twist the facts and convince a jury of something that is not even remotely true. Lawyers who sue insurance companies know that they have an inside edge with the natural prejudice most people feel against insurance companies. All they have to do is say that the insurance company is just trying to deprive that poor insured or claimant of the money he is rightfully entitled to receive and they are on the way to winning their case.

The sad truth is that insurance fraud is not a priority in this country. The police and prosecuting authorities are quick to pursue a bank robber or burglar, but getting them to commit the resources to investigate an insurance fraud case is an uphill battle. Arson, for instance, is the least often and least effectively prosecuted crime in America. Most insurance-fraud cases are circumstantial in nature and lack direct proof in the form of eyewitnesses. Those are not the kinds of cases the police and prosecutors want to readily pursue, because they know it will be a lengthy investigation, perhaps a costly investigation, and the prospects of conviction are far less than any other type of crime. So most of the time, we have to go it on our own. Sometimes we have to even go up against them at trial when a local fire investigator says that it was not a case of arson but an electrical short, or when the police quickly close an investigation without even identifying any suspects. When a jury hears about those things, the job becomes even tougher.

Many states have insurance-fraud departments charged with the investigation of insurance-fraud cases. But in virtually every jurisdiction, they are under-staffed and over-worked. Many states have only ten or twelve public investigators charged with the investigation of insurance fraud in a state where there may be tens of thousands of suspected fraudulent claims. Unless they have a case where somebody has been caught red-handed or has confessed to the crime, it may never be fully investigated. Once again, we are left on our own.

The great irony is that while insurance fraud is widely perceived as a victimless crime, it is far from victimless. The average burglary results in the theft of about $1,000 in property. The average arson results in damage of over $100,000. While everybody believes that burglary is a serious crime that must be prevented and prosecuted, the same cannot be said for the perception of insurance-fraud cases. While the typical burglary may have one victim, the typical insurance-fraud case leaves us all as victims. It is estimated that over 20 percent of the premiums we all pay for insurance in this country goes to fraudulent claims. In some areas of the country, the numbers are even higher. So all of us pay for insurance fraud whenever we pay for our insurance premiums. We are all the victims of insurance fraud.

The fact is that even most insurance companies are not fully committed to the fight against insurance fraud. While most insurance companies have investigators on staff, few of them dedicate enough manpower and resources to handle the volume of claims that require investigation. As a result, without some clear indication that something positive will result from the investigation, many cases are quickly closed and never fully investigated. Resources for following up on investigations by tracking down witnesses and obtaining records are limited, which makes the process even more difficult. The challenges in this business are everywhere.

So why do I love my job? It is not the money, that's for sure. While some of us are well paid for our work, none of us is getting rich. It's not the workplace, either. We have to go to places where even the police are afraid to go. We meet with people who are dangerous, and we do so without a badge or a gun on our hip to protect us. We deal with people who are often driven to insurance fraud out of desperation and desperate people are capable of anything. I have been threatened more times than I can count. I have had guns pointed at me more often than I care to remember. I have questioned my sanity for going to some of the places I have gone to complete an investigation, but I love this job because it gives me the opportunity to face all of these challenges and still find the truth. It is rewarding to come to the end of an investigation and realize you have uncovered the truth. While some of the people we meet with are not the ones you would want to bring home for dinner, every case is a different story and every time there is something new to learn. And behind it all, those who do this work know that we are in the unique position of being able to make sure that the right decision is made whatever it may be.

This book has some of my favorite cases from over the years. The facts are real and so are the people. The names have been changed to protect the innocent and in some cases to protect the guilty—or, to be more precise, to protect me from being sued by one of those people who doesn't like his story being told in a book. These are the real stories of my cases and my work as an investigator. I hope that you will enjoy these stories and will learn something about the work that I do.

DETECTION OF DECEPTION IN INTERVIEWING

I teach a course called "Interviewing Techniques and the Detection of Deception in Investigations."

I will refer to this many times during the course of this book. I use several different techniques to tell if someone is lying to me. I can usually tell if someone is lying to me after approximately five minutes. The following is a list of the techniques I use and teach:

1. Neurolinguistics

2. The Reid Technique

3. Stan Walters, "the lie guy"

4. Micro expressions

5. SCAN (scientific content analysis)

6. Mirroring

7. Concealment vs. Falsification

8. Kinetics or Kinesis (body language)

Neurolinguistics is the study of neural mechanisms in the human brain that control comprehension and language. The Reid Technique teaches the student to observe a combination of body language and specific words a suspect uses to detect deception. Stan Walters (the lie guy) teaches a class he developed by interviewing convicted felons. Stan developed this class by conducting a study of the felons, also studying their body language, to see what they did when he knew they were lying. The study of a person's micro expressions is a technique developed by Dr. Paul Ekman that is extremely useful. SCAN (Scientific Content Analysis) was developed by Avinoam Sapir, a former agent with the Israeli Mossad. SCAN is technique based on the study of verbs, pronouns, sentence structure, paragraph structure, and the changes in these that occur during a potentially deceptive person's interview. SCAN also involves the study of body language, but in a very different way, dealing with deceptive human behavior and the difference from normal human behavior. Mirroring is a technique that continues to fascinate me. Using this technique, you are able to invade a person's mind and develop a rapport with them that can be very useful.

Concealment vs. Falsification is a technique where you force the interviewee that is concealing information into a verifiable falsification statement.

I have taken almost every course that exists on deception. I would suggest that everyone who reads this book attend as many of these classes and seminars that they can to increase their knowledge of detection of deception. It is a fascinating field of study. There is also a book called *Detecting Lies and Deceit*, written by Aldert Vrij, which is also extremely useful and intriguing.

I use all of these techniques every day in my interviewing, but I do not use everything that is taught in each course. Some of the theories work and some do not work. Some are easy to use, and others are impossible to use while you are interviewing someone face-to-face. How I discovered what worked and what did not was a process of elimination. When I would try a new technique, if it worked I would continue to use it; if it didn't work, it got discarded from my bag of tricks.

Out of all of the different techniques, I probably use SCAN the most.

I have mastered detection of deception through thirty-four years of interviewing people on my current job and ten years as a state trooper. I have tried all of these techniques, and I know which ones work. I do have to admit that as a state trooper, I used to cheat a little. For example, many times the computer at the post would be down, and I had no way of verifying a stolen car's plate or serial number. That didn't stop me. I would still pull over potentially stolen vehicles. I would simply handcuff the occupants, put them into the back seat of my cruiser, and tell them I had to do an inspection of their vehicle. I would then turn on an old-fashioned reel tape recorder that I had hidden under my seat with a wired microphone on the gear shift. I would then leave them alone for about ten minutes, acting like I was inspecting their vehicle. When I returned to the car, their faces would be all flushed and they would appear to be very nervous. I would simply sit in the driver's seat, take out the tape recorder, and play it back for them. Most of the time the conversation would be something like this: "Do you think he knows we stole it? What are we going to do if he finds out?" "Keep your cool, I don't think he knows!" "I told you we would get in trouble; this is the last time I ever listen to you!" I would simply turn around, look at them sweating in the back seat, and say, "Boys, you're under arrest for auto theft." That was back in the early seventies, before the laws came out concerning taping of conversations prior to you not being a party to the conversation. That brings up another hurdle that insurance investigators have to overcome. We cannot lie to anyone, but the police can, and sometimes it makes their job a lot easier.

In the last thirty-four years I have interviewed hundreds of people, and when I concluded a case where I was positive someone lied to me, I would look back and determine when they lied and what they did while lieing. I made a mental note of each of these, and I started seeing a pattern of things people do when they lie or conceal information.

I mentioned earlier in my list a technique called mirroring. This is a unique way to get into someone's head, and they don't even know you are there. If it is used correctly on the right person under the right circumstances, you will get a confession every time. Mirroring goes back to the old thought of subliminal suggestion. If you are old enough to remember going to an outdoor drive-in movie, they were played on reel-to-reels, with individual frames. On the reel were many frames that would roll past the projector light and thus your image of the frames would appear on the large screen. It is a proven fact that if the theatre would splice in a few frames of popcorn, pop, candy, etc., right before intermission, you would see the frame of the popcorn in your mind but not actually see it with your eyes. This would provoke an instant memory recollection. When they had intermission, whatever they put on the single frames, the sales of popcorn, pop or candy would increase approximately 500 percent, because in your subliminal mind it was suggested and you could not help yourself.

The same principle works in the mirroring technique.

When I first meet with someone I think is guilty of insurance fraud or is lying to me, I use the mirroring principle. First, you wait for the person to initiate some type of body language. It can be anything—rubbing the nose, crossing the arms, crossing the legs, leaning an elbow on the table or desk, putting one hand over a forearm or whatever. I wait for the person to do something kinetic, and then I wait about thirty seconds and imitate them. This might go on for thirty minutes, and when they change to another movement, I will also wait about thirty seconds to start imitating them again. After about ten to fifteen times of imitating them, I will stop. I then wait a few minutes and make some type of movement—crossing my arms, folding my hands together etc. If the person is ready for mirroring, I will see them imitate me within thirty seconds. I will then continue to change positions and actions about ten times, and if they continue to mimic me, I have them, I am in their mind, and they completely trust me.

After the person imitates you back several times, you then stop, very sincerely reach out and touch the person's forearm, and say, "John, is there something you want to tell me?" If you see the person's head rise to the ceiling, this is a three-stage process of a confession that is coming. The first phase of looking to the ceiling is, "God, help me." The second stage is an exhalation of air that you will hear. This is the stress of having this load on their shoulders about to be lifted off. The third stage is when the person's chin drops to the chest.

You know at this point that the person is ready to confess, but right before they do, they will reach over and touch your forearm back, just like you touched them. It is not a heavy touch, but a very light one, and they may do this several times. Why does a person confess to someone when they really don't want to? It is because you have developed a rapport with the person and they trust you. I tell everyone I teach who tries this technique or anyone who gets someone to confess, the one thing you never do is be judgmental. If you are judgmental, the person will turn on you and possibly even attack you because you have violated the trust and rapport that was established during the interview while mirroring.

I always say something like this: "John thanks for being honest with me. I don't approve of what you did, but I do understand why you did it. If my back was against the wall like yours, I might have done the same thing myself. That doesn't make what you did right, but I understand. Now let's see how I can help you get through this problem and see what we might do to lessen it or possibly even make it go away. I can't promise anything, but I will do my best."

Never lie to the person by making promises you cannot keep. Just tell them you will help them in any way that you can.

Concealment vs. Falsification is another useful technique that I earlier described on the list. This technique is used by asking additional questions where the person has intentionally concealed information that you cannot verify. A very simple example of this is if you ask someone a question and it is, "Who were you with on the night of the fire?" and they answer, "Bill and Bob." You can let that go or forgive them for not telling you the last names. You need to ask them what Bill and Bob's last names are, their addresses, phone numbers, etc. This will force them to make up more lies if Bill and Bob were fabricated names to conceal information from you.

The last technique on the list is Kinetics. I use this technique every day in my interviewing. It involves the things that a person starts doing when they are under stress or lying that they do not do normally in their baseline. These are specific things such as: rubbing their nose, a slight shoulder bump, belching, moving their butt from side to side in their chair before or after answering a question, hesitations, shaking their head no but saying yes with their voice, increase in eye blinks, uncontrolled laughter, a fake smile, crossing or uncrossing their arms, legs, or feet when they had not done this before, tapping of the foot, putting their hand over their mouth when answering a question, and the absence of snot running from their nose when they are crying.

I mentioned in the start of this chapter that I have developed a class that I teach all over the country to other SIU investigators, state employees, police officers, insurance organizations, IRS investigators, Alcohol, Tobacco and Firearms agents, FBI, liquor agents, arson investigators, attorneys, and state fraud investigators. I call this class "Detection of Deception in Interviewing." I teach in the class what I call 100 per centers, or things that people do when they lie. In this book I will refer to them as KDIs, or Key Deception Indicators. When you see someone do one KDI, you become alerted. When they do two KDIs, your eyebrows will go up. If they do three or more, you have a real problem at that point in the interview and the person is being deceptive to you. I call these a double or triple whammy!

Before I interview someone, I will ask them questions that have nothing to do with the investigation in order to establish what I call a "baseline."

This baseline is unique to the person I am speaking with. I ask them their prior addresses; I ask those personal questions about their grandchildren's pictures in their living room. When I worked the southern states, I would always ask, "So where did you get this velvet painting of Elvis?" It doesn't matter what you ask them about, as long as it is something of importance to them. I want you to think of your own living room or family room and think about what you have on display. You put the objects there for a reason. You want people to appreciate them as much as you do, but how many people who come to your home ever actually comment on them?

That is where I start building rapport with the person I am about to interview. When I arrive, they have their guard up. I am the bad person from the insurance company who is there to deny their claim or try to send them to jail. The rapport when I arrive is nonexistent. They also think that adjusters and investigators get extra pay for claims that are denied or paid less than the claim is worth, and there is absolutely no truth to this.

I try to change that within the first five minutes.

I teach in my classes that if the student will use the baseline and rapport-building techniques that I teach, that they can tell if someone is lying to them within a short period of time after establishing the baseline and actually starting the interview.

Once you see something that someone has in their house that is of importance, all you have to do is comment on it, and they will probably talk about the item for five to ten minutes. When they stop talking about it, you can ask a couple questions about what they said, and this just adds to the rapport building because you are interested in what they have said. Usually when I go to someone's home, they immediately want me to go into their living room. This is the last place I want to be. The reason for this is that in order to establish control, develop rapport, and have a successful interview, I need to be four feet away from the person. In a living room, you are about ten to twelve feet away from the person, and this is way too far. Rather than the living room, always try to persuade to person to let you conduct the interview in the kitchen. The kitchen is not only a comfortable place where you take your family and friends, but the kitchen table is an ideal distance to have a successful interview.

I need to go over one more time, step by step, how I get to the person's kitchen table. This is very important. When I arrive at the person's home, I am always on time. I am always prepared. I have researched the entire claim file, and I have gone over every piece of evidence and information in the file. I have all of my questions written out ahead of time and numbered. I have all of the forms needed that I have to have the person sign. I have all of the equipment I need to complete the interview—audio recorder, forms, pen, calculator, claim file, questions, camera, etc.

I had a case in Alabama once where an elderly woman, Anita, had actually seen the person leaving our insured's house with a gas can shortly before the house exploded into flamed. Anita had been interviewed by the police, and she refused to speak to them because she "didn't want to get involved."

I went to Anita's door, and introduced myself to her. She stated that she had already spoken to several police officers and wanted nothing to do with the case. I told Anita that I understood her concern, the possible retaliation of the person who had done this, and her reluctance to speak to anyone. At that moment I looked into her living room, and I saw a quilt rack. All I did was comment, "Did you make those?" She said yes and immediately opened the door. You have to be very sincere about the interest you show in whatever you make a comment about. Anita asked me in (a total stranger) and walked toward the quilts. She said that she had made the quilts and asked me if I would like to see the rest of them. I said yes, and she proceeded for the next hour to show me all of her quilts, bringing about twenty of them, one at a time, from another room.

The reason I am telling you this story is two-fold. The first reason is that because I asked Anita about the quilts, she eventually gave me the name of the person who set the fire. I gave this information to the police, the subject was arrested, and, as far as I know, is still in jail. You wonder if I took advantage of an elderly woman and put her life in jeopardy. I did not; Anita remained a confidential informant, and when the subject was confronted, he confessed.

Even if the subject had not confessed, I would never have given her up as the person who "ratted" him out, because I had promised her I would not. I always tell any person who gives me confidential information that the only way I would give them up if I was ordered to by a judge, and I would probably go to jail to keep any of my informants from getting hurt.

Why do you think she gave me this information? Anita trusted me because I took the time to develop a rapport with her, which no one else had done. It also is because many people are just lonely and they just want to talk to you.

Like I discussed earlier, when I use this technique, it doesn't have to be quilts, but anything personal to the subject. It can be anything, bowling trophies, Hummel collections, thimble collections, or gun collections.

My point is that it doesn't matter what the item is, all you have to do is recognize what the person has out on display and all you have to do is comment on it. If they want to tell you about it, you have broken the ice, so to speak, and after that all you have to do is let them go on talking. Sometimes it is ten minutes; sometimes it is an hour or two. When they are done talking, you take there. The rapport has been established, and the trust ╷ere as long as you don't violate the trust in some way. when I get to this point, I ask the person if we can go into the╷ ╷tchen. At the kitchen table, you can observe the subject's body language more clearly.

As an example, when I watch someone, say the Anita with the quilts, I observe her normal body language and behavior when she is telling me about how she made the quilts, how many children she has, how long was it since her husband had passed away, etc. When I start asking them questions during the interview, such as *where were you on the night of the fire?*, I watch for a change in their emotions, their eye blinks, their body movements, looking up to the right or the left, how many times they touch their nose or cross their legs or arms, hesitations, long, ahh's. I also observe their resting body language, for example, when they are simply sitting there and do not know how to answer the question.

I have also been teaching student's one tip that is very easy to develop rapport when you first meet with a subject. Take an extra two to three seconds, and while you are shaking their hand, look into their eyes long enough to say to yourself, they have brown eyes or blue eyes. This will help you develop rapport at an accelerated rate. Also, if you get a chance to just touch the person, on the shoulder or arm, this is a huge asset and will help you break down barriers.

I learned a long time ago, that "the truth is the truth, and a lie is a lie." When I interview someone, I usually have the advantage of already reviewing what they told their insurance agent about a claim, what they told the police, and what they told our claims adjuster before I actually sit down and interview them. I look for consistency in their statement. If I start seeing discrepancies in their statements, I know something is wrong, because "the truth is the truth, and a lie is a lie."

When I teach my classes, I use a short exercise to show the class that Neurolinguistics does in fact work. I have the class write down the first two colors that come to their mind. Let's try it. Stop reading this book, get a pencil and paper, and write down the first two colors that come to your mind, and then come back to the book. Don't look at the next paragraph until you have written down the two colors.

Hey, I said not to look!

The result will be hard to prove to you because you are probably by yourself and I usually do this in a classroom of two to three hundred people. Eighty-five percent of people will write down red and blue. Ten percent will write down a combination with red or blue, such as red and yellow or blue and green, but the red or blue will be there. Five percent of the people who take this test will not write down red or blue in any way, and I always single them out in the class and tell them that this means that they are just weird! (This usually gets a pretty good laugh from the class, and the 5 percent take it in a joking way).

This is a good time to discuss another issue that baffles me and has for years. I was told in a SCAN (Scientific Content Analysis) class I attended, taught by Avinoam Sapir, that "everyone wants to tell everyone everything." If this is true, why doesn't every criminal tell the police what happened when they are interviewed, or why doesn't every person who commits insurance fraud confess to me immediately when I interview them? The answer is that even though "everyone wants to tell everyone everything," there is the fear of punishment that keeps them from telling you everything.

If you want to test this, the next time you are on a plane, ask the person seated next to you how they are doing and just wait. They will tell you their entire life story. People do this because they know they will never see you again.

Another 100 "percenter," or KDI, that I have been teaching recently is the shoulder bump. The shoulder bump is an extremely quick movement of the upper shoulders. It happens so fast you need to watch for this very closely, and it usually happens multiple times. I was watching TV with my wife, and a woman appeared on TV stating that her foster son had been abducted. I watched her for thirty seconds, and in that time period she did the shoulder bump seven times. I told my wife that she had killed the child. Two weeks later she was arrested for the killing and mutilation of the child's body. I think out of all of the techniques that I teach, the shoulder bump is the most reliable, other than answering a question with a question.

One of the other most useful KDIs is the absence of snot when someone starts crying in an interview. Avinoam Sapir teaches that you cannot have a real cry without snot.

If you ever get a chance, you should watch the infamous Susan Smith in her original TV interview about her two boys being missing before she was arrested. Look at Susan's smile—it only went up to the sides of her mouth (fake smile)—and when she cried, she had no snot. I taught this technique to a class of adjusters from my company. One girl, Denise, had a terrible phone call two weeks after the class. Her brother had been murdered in his bed. He was in the Marine Corps and the police department had no leads to his murderer. Denise went to the funeral and observed her sister-in-law crying. She also observed that there was no snot. Denise went to the local police department after the funeral and asked if any of the detectives there had SCAN training. One said he had and how could he help her.

Denise relayed the story of her sister-in-law not having any snot. The detective immediately started focusing his case on the wife of Denise's brother. The investigation later revealed that the wife had a boyfriend and the boyfriend had killed Denise's brother so they could run away together. The boyfriend also admitted later that during the next week or so after the funeral of Denise's brother, he had planned to kill his wife so that he and Denise's sister-in-law could run away together with no ties. This case was solved, two people went to jail for life, and one murder was prevented because of the lack of snot!

At this point, I need to explain KDIs, what they are, how they work, and why they are useful in detecting deception.

These are the KDIs or Key Deception Indicators:

1. Dry mouth: When you lie, the saliva flow stops in your mouth and your mouth will become dry. You will start licking your lips and start swallowing in an attempt to get the saliva flow starting again.

2. Nose: You will rub or scratch your nose when you lie. There are erectile tissue or nerve endings in your nose that become irritated when you lie, due to the increase in blood pressure. You have no choice but to rub or scratch your nose.

3. Stomach growl: When you lie, the gastric juices in your stomach start flowing and you can hear the stomach growl, or the person will experience acid reflux and sometimes will actually have the symptoms of having to throw up.

4. The shoulder bump: When you lie, you will raise your shoulders slightly. It is hard to detect, but if you watch for it, you will see several shoulder bumps in succession when a person lies.

5. The butt slide: When someone lies, they will slide their butt in their chair to one side or the other just before the lie or after. If you see a double butt slide, this is huge!

6. Eye blinks: When you lie, the eye blinks will increase from one blink every eight seconds to one every second.

7. Hand to head: When you lie, your hand will go to your head in some fashion right before the lie or after—to the neck, face, ear, hair, chin, nose, etc.

8. Hesitations: When you ask someone a question and there is a hesitation or an "uh,, or ahhhhhhhhhh," this is deception. They are trying to come up with answer that is fabricated, and they need time to think.

9. The backslash: For example, when someone says, "She was/is a good person." The backslash is when the brain goes into a protection mode. The first word is past tense, and the brain said, "Oops!" If you say "was" and you are talking about a person who is missing, it's a mistake. You should have said "is," and most likely, you know that the missing person is dead, by referring to them in the past tense. I will discuss this later and use examples from the Scott Peterson case.

10. Question with a question: If I ask someone, "Did you set this fire?" and they answer, "Did I set this fire?" this is a question with a question and they are being deceptive.

11. Confession: If a person looks up, sighs, and then the chin drops to the chest, he is ready to confess.

12. Changes in verbs, pronouns, sentence structure, or paragraphs out of place—"the" wife versus "my" wife.

13. No snot!

14. Flight-or-fight syndrome.

15. The punishment question: If a person is lenient toward the person who set their house on fire when they are asked, "What should happen to the person who did set their house on fire?" they probably are guilty of arson. If they want severe punishment, then they are probably innocent.

16. Time reversal: This is when a subject gives a statement narrative first from morning to night. Then you ask the person to repeat the narrative from night to morning. The narrative should be the same. If the person is being deceptive, they cannot relay the facts in reverse order because

they have only rehearsed it from the morning to the night version.

17. Small wrinkles in the center of the forehead: This is an indicator of deception by the person.

18. Steepling: This is when the person you are interviewing steeples their hands in front of them, pressing all five of their fingertips together. When the person steeples you, they are telling you that they think they are better than you, superior to you, and are trying to gain control of the interview.

19. Folded arm lean: This is when a subject who has been sitting erect with their arms down suddenly folds their arms across their chest and leans back in their chair. This is another way of the subject trying to gain control of the interview and that you are powerless.

In the chapters ahead, I will be referring to all of these various KDIs that helped me in solving various cases.

THE STOLEN, FOUND JEWELRY

This case investigation was very time consuming and occurred in a southern town.

One item of reference that I would like the reader to understand is that under an insurance policy, any jewelry has a limit of payment under the policy. If you have a very expensive piece of jewelry, or many items of jewelry, they need to be specifically insured. If you do not have the item scheduled, you probably only have $2,500 coverage on all of your jewelry if you have a theft or fire.

The scheduled policy then covers the jewelry for anything—loss, theft, fire, etc.

I wish that no one would have ever written this type of policy, because if fraud has been committed, it is the hardest to prove.

This insured's name was "Jane." Jane claimed that someone broke into her home using a credit card on a metal door of her garage. They entered her home and stole all of her expensive jewelry that was scheduled for $50,000.

Jane was a professional and lived in a very nice apartment. She had recently been involved in a bitter divorce. In most investigations, insured's are very cooperative, and they want me to try to get back their stolen items and find out who stole the items. They feel that they have been violated and usually want revenge in some way.

Jane was very uncooperative from the start, and this raised a red flag immediately. This is typical of a claim that could possibly be fraudulent.

Jane questioned why were even investigating the theft and demanded a check immediately. Jane was also very emphatic that her former husband was the person responsible for the theft. After you read the conclusion of this investigation, I think you will feel as I do that this is one of the funniest claims I have ever investigated.

I agreed to meet with Jane at her apartment. Right away she was hostile and said she needed to show me how the thief (her former husband) got into her apartment. She stated that someone had used a credit card to enter her garage door. She said she had seen this occur on TV (*CSI*) and knew that was how they got into her apartment. The door was a heavily constructed metal door. I tried several times, with Jane present; to open the door with a credit card, and it was impossible.

During the course of my career, I have been to several locksmith schools and many auto theft schools where we were instructed how to tell if a door lock or the ignition switch of a car had been violated. I formed a baseline on Jane within five minutes of meeting with her, and I knew that her entire claim was a lie. Here's why: Jane looked up and to the left when she lied, she rubbed her nose constantly, and every time I asked her a question, she would slightly bump her shoulders. Jane's eye blinks were also so fast that I could not count them when she was answering my serious questions.

During the baseline (what is normal for that person), she looked up and to the right when she was remembering or recalling, and she exhibited no other signs of deception at that point as I discussed earlier.

Jane then stated that she had "preserved" evidence in her garage that the thief had left. She proceeded to show me a trashcan in the middle of the garage that someone had defecated in, and the evidence was still there, after several weeks. The "thief" had taken boxes of photos and slides of the insured and her son, put them in the bottom of the trashcan, and somehow managed to hike themselves up, straddle the trashcan, and literally defecate in it. I am still to this day trying to get that visual out of my head.

The ironic thing about this situation is that the insured demanded that the police take the evidence and have it DNA tested to prove that her husband was the one who had defecated in the trash can. Naturally, the police refused to take the evidence. At this point, I should also make you aware that there were many items in the garage that a normal burglar would take, and nothing was missing in the garage or even the first floor of the house.

I took photos of the evidence but did not bag it.

The insured then took me upstairs. The house was a tri-level with the garage on the ground floor, the kitchen and living room on the second floor, and the bedroom and bath on the third floor. There were many items of value on the second floor that should have been taken, and items in the kitchen and living room and dining room would have been a burglar's paradise. If this seems strange to you, good, because it also seemed very strange to me. In all the years I have been an investigator, I have never seen a burglar bypass expensive items in the living room just to get to other items in the house. Jane and I went into her kitchen, where we started a recorded interview.

We were halfway through the statement when I discovered that Jane and her former husband had just filed bankruptcy and there were several outstanding suits against each of them. She blamed her husband for everything and attempted to clothe herself as the angelic type whose husband had wronged her. Jane knew that he was the one that came into her house, defecated on her photos in the trashcan, and then went to her bedroom and stole her jewelry (that he had given to her).

Next we need to discuss the husband (John) and his relationship with Jane. I met with John before meeting with Jane. He was a real interesting character. John had remarried and had also filed a claim with us about his Jane stealing contents from his house. He had an eyewitness who saw Jane pull up to the garage and fill up a truck with items from his house—TVs, stereo, DVD player, furniture, etc. His claim was also nearly $50,000. I checked the policy for the house, and Jane's name was still on the policy. John was upset when I told him that there was no coverage because of this, and in the insurance world you cannot steal from yourself.

I was intrigued by John because when I told him that Jane had accused him of breaking into her apartment, putting all of the family photos in her trashcan, and then defecating on them and stealing all of her jewelry, he just laughed.

I remember him saying, "Why would I steal her items when I knew she had insurance and she would just collect the money back?" From that point on, I saw no deception in his statement and believed John fully.

John went on to say that even though Jane was an anesthesiologist, she was really nuts. He went on to say that his ex-wife had showed symptoms of paranoia and that was one of the reasons for their divorce. He also said, "I don't know where she lives now, and I don't want to know. In fact, I hope I never see her again!" I believed what he said.

John verified that he had purchased the jewelry for her at various times in their marriage. He told me of a witness who saw Jane taking his items from his house when he was on vacation. The witness, Fred, proved to be one of the most interesting people I have ever met (other than a CIA hit-man I will introduce you to in a later chapter). The witness proved to be a neighbor of John's who lived two houses down. The geography of the neighborhood must be explained for the next part of my story.

The neighborhood was in the outskirts of a town that we will call Monroe. The area was wooded with a small river running behind the insured's and his neighbor's property. I went to visit Fred. After I took a statement from him about Jane, her moving truck, and taking all of John's items, we got to talking. It was late in the day, and we had developed a rapport. He offered me a drink, and surprisingly, he drank the same thing I do, a Cuba Libre, so we had a couple—well, maybe three. It was late in the day and my last appointment, if my boss is reading this.

I told him about being a former Marine, Vietnam, being a police officer, and told him some of my war stories. Fred said, "Would you like to see some of my guns?" I really started to like this guy now. Fred had an arsenal of fully automatic weapons that would make an army surplus store jealous. He brought out a few, loaded them up, and I got to shoot some amazing weapons that I had never even heard of. The weapons had no manufacturer and no serial numbers, which made me very suspicious of what he did for a living before he retired. We spent the next several hours shooting into the river at rocks behind his home, and it was very enjoyable to say the least, because I am sort of a gun enthusiast myself. Fred let me fire a 9-mm, which was sort of like an Uzi, had a thirty-round magazine, and the magazine was empty in about three seconds with no recoil. I wish I could buy one of these at a local gun store. I think he said it was made in Germany. Fred, if you're reading this, thanks for an enjoyable afternoon.

Fred told me that he was still friends with both John and Jane but he liked John better because Jane was a little crazy. Fred verified that Jane pulled up with a small moving van and carried many items out of the garage. He had been told by John that Jane would be coming by to get some items, so he didn't think anything about it. Fred said that he saw her carrying out TVs, couches, etc., and he thought, *Wow, John is getting his clock cleaned in this divorce*, but he didn't think it was any of his business. It turned out later, when speaking with John, that Jane was supposed to get four or five boxes of items in the garage, and instead she cleaned out the house. I should note that all of these items were in Jane's home when I went there to interview her.

Let's get back to the actual interview of the ex-wife, which proved to be one of the most interesting claims I have had.

I finally got down the real issue of the claim, and this was the jewelry itself. I asked Jane where the jewelry was in the home prior to it being stolen. She stated that it was upstairs in her bedroom.

It should be noted that prior to the interview with Jane, when I interviewed John, he had a clear alibi on the night of the reported theft. He also denied having any key to Jane's apartment. He said that he felt as though the claim was totally bogus and Jane was trying to rip our insurance company off.

When Jane told me that her jewelry had been upstairs in her bedroom, I asked her if she would show me where. Being the lady that she was, she immediately took offense to this and said that it would be improper for her to take me upstairs to her bedroom. I kept the recorder running to protect myself from any allegations that she may make later.

I assured her that it was strictly business. We got upstairs, and I asked her where in the bedroom she had the jewelry prior to the theft. She advised that the jewelry was in her middle dresser drawer.

I asked her to open the drawer, and she said there was no need for that; all that was in there was costume jewelry.

I asked her again to open the drawer because I wanted to see where the jewelry had been. Jane stated that the jewelry had been in a jewelry bag and several times objected to opening the drawer. I again insisted. She finally opened the drawer, I took a photo of the contents, and she hurriedly closed the drawer.

I asked Jane to reopen the drawer, and that again raised objections. She finally did re-open the drawer, and my curiosity was piqued by a jewelry bag that I had seen in the drawer when she opened it. I asked Jane what was in the jewelry bag, and she again said it was just costume jewelry.

What happened next was unexpected and pretty bizarre.

It took me about four times to get Jane to take the bag out, and she finally did.

I asked her to open the bag and place the contents on her bed. Reluctantly she did so. She held the bag above the bed, and as the jewelry was falling to the bed, she said in a very loud and excited voice, "Thank you, God! I have found my jewelry!"

At that point I didn't think that God had anything to do with this miraculous recovery of the items. I photographed all of the jewelry and made an inventory describing each piece and verified with her that these were the items worth $50,000 that she had been claiming and were scheduled on her insurance policy.

I sat down and finished the interview with Jane. I told her that in my opinion she had committed an attempted insurance fraud and I would have to report this to the authorities. She argued that the entire thing was a mistake, and I told her that I didn't think it was.

I then drove to the local police department with a burglary detective, explained what Jane had attempted to do, and that she had tried to steal $50,000 from our company.

The police detective took offense to what Jane had attempted. He asked for a copy of my file, and he eventually took the case to the prosecutor. The case went before the grand jury, and Jane was indicted for attempted insurance fraud. When I was on the stand testifying, the prosecutor asked me to explain to the jury what happened on the date and time that I was at the insured's home when she presented her claim for $50,000.

When I got to the point of the jewelry bag being raised in the air before it hit the bed, I could not wait to look at the jury while they were absorbing what I was saying. I still think they were shocked about the human waste in the trash can when I hit them with the, "Oh, thank you, God" issue that the insured had so dramatically voiced when the jewelry hit the bed.

I do want to state that all of the jewelry that the insured was claiming was in the bag, which was on top of all the other jewelry in her drawer.

When I looked at the jury, I could read their faces and saw a very strong guilty verdict approaching. When the case was concluded and the case went to the jury, it did not take very long for them to reach a decision.

Normally if you get a verdict in four to eight hours, this is good. The jury was out for about a half hour and came back with a guilty verdict against Jane.

The look of shock on Jane's face was amazing to me. She actually believed that the jury would come back with a not guilty. I never could understand her mental state at that time.

The judge was not very forgiving, and she got two years in jail and three years probation.

I wonder if she ever thanked God for anything again that he didn't give to her.

TESTIFYING IN THE COURTROOM

I mentioned earlier that I have testified at trials many times over the course of my career. Jurors are very interesting people. I do think that there are some citizens that truly care about serving on a jury and they think that it is their duty to do so, and I commend them for this.

I have discovered that during any trial, a person is not found innocent or guilty based on the evidence alone.

It has more to do with who is more believable, the attorney for the insured, the attorney for the insurance company, the witnesses, the SIU investigator, etc. There is another factor with juries that I use all of the time. When you get called into a courtroom, you know that all eyes are on you—the judge, jury, court reporter, bailiff, spectators, insured, and the attorneys. They are all looking at you walking in, the way you are dressed, and your demeanor. Everything about you comes into play. I always walk in standing straight and confident, sure of the case. This lets the jurors know that this is not the first time you have done this, and it helps with your later testimony. I also turn to the judge, either nod or say hello, and then turn to the jury and make eye contact with them. This is the most important part of your entry. If you don't look at the jury and actually make eye contact with each juror and nod to them, they feel that you have something you are hiding or you do not want to be there.

Another thing I do always is answer every question, whether the question is from our attorney or the insured's attorney, the same way, with the same voice pitch, and I never get upset. If I say "yes sir" to my attorney, then I address the other attorney the same way. If you don't, the jury can see right through this, and they form an opinion that you don't like the other attorney and hold that against you later in the jury room.

Many times you will run into an insured's attorney who is less than honorable. They will start badgering you on the stand about one or two issues to try and trip you up. They want you to say something without thinking about your answer, because once the words come out of your mouth, the jury puts that in their mind. If a judge tells them to not consider something that was said after our attorney wins an objection, the words spoken are still in their mind when they go to deliberation and usually will not be disregarded as the judge ordered.

The way that I avoid traps from an insured's attorney is two-fold. First, I never answer the question right away; I think about my answer and then give an answer. If the insured's attorney wants to really trip you up, they will ask a very long question, or one that has two questions hidden in one question, three to four minutes long.. I will wait for them to finish and then wait a few seconds and then say, "Can you repeat that? I didn't understand your question." This usually causes the insured's attorney to go into a rampage of insults and demeaning statements about my intelligence. They will say to me, "What didn't you understand about the question? Any fool could understand that!" They are usually yelling at me when saying this.

At this point I calmly look at the judge and ask him to please advise the insured's attorney not to yell at me. I then say, "I have a hearing problem sometimes. I was wounded in Vietnam from a very large explosion, more than once, and my hearing is not very good, I am sorry."

The insured's attorney knows right away he just screwed up, and the jurors do not like him very much at this point. I do not make this statement to the judge to get sympathy for an untruthful statement. I was wounded in Vietnam twice, received two Purple Hearts, and was around many explosions, etc. My hearing is getting worse all of the time, and it was a result of combat, but it is still fun to use at trial.

A jury will give a verdict to the side that they think is telling the truth or the side that they like the best. They are supposed to weigh the evidence before rendering a decision, but that is not always the case.

I have another suggestion about testifying in court that I teach to all of my classes. Everyone is under a lot of stress when they go into a courtroom. I don't care how many times you testify, the butterflies are always there. Body language teaches us that when someone is under stress, the stress has to leak out in some type of body movement, gesture, or physical reaction. To eliminate this body language of stress being seen by a jury, I teach everyone to take a pen (one that doesn't make any noise when you click it) with them to the stand and cup it in the palm of your left hand. (You need the right hand empty because you have to hold that hand up when swearing to tell the truth.) After you are sworn in and you take your seat, you start clicking the pen repeatedly; no one will hear it because you use a pen that doesn't make any noise. This will release all of your emotions and stress into the pen instead of the stress being released in your body movements or "leakage."

I developed these techniques by watching Saddam Hussein when he was being interviewed by Dan Rather just prior to the US invasion of his country. He had a pen in front of him but no paper during the interview, and when things became stressful, the pen disappeared below the table. This relieved his stress.

Nervousness is usually equated with lying. You may be telling the total truth, but you could come off as being a liar instead if you show signs of stress to the jury. If you ever get called to testify at a trial, remember to take a quiet clicking pen with you. I use it all of the time.

I have seen jury's do unbelievable things. You think you have a case won, and the case goes totally in the opposite direction. I have cases where I thought I had lost and ended up winning.

The one person in the courtroom that knows a jury is the court bailiff. I always try to establish a rapport with the bailiff. They sit through trials every day and they can read jury's just based on their expressions and demeanor during the trial. I always have the bailiff give me thumb up or thumb down during the course of the trail so I know where I stand.

Cases are not won on evidence. I have seen this way too many times. Jurors are paid about ten dollars per day to be away from their jobs and family, sit through long hours of testimony, and then have to make a decision based on their feelings and what they believe or do not believe.

It is up to me to convince a jury that I am the good guy and the insured is the bad guy in every case that I take to trial.

Another hint that I teach is when you answer a question, do not look at the person who asked you the question when answering; look at the jury. Keep your eyes on the person while they are asking the question, then before you answer, turn your body to the jury and answer to them. Rapport and believability are the keys to your testimony.

I will never take a case to a jury trial unless I know I can win the case. I have testified in hundreds of trials and can only remember losing one jury trial in thirty-four years, and that was a trial by a judge and not a jury.

GETTING AWAY WITH MURDER

One of the strangest and most interesting claims I ever worked involved a large contracting firm. To protect the innocent, I will say this occurred in Indiana.

I received a call about large fire in a major city. The fire had started at about midnight, and the building and all of its contents had been destroyed. This claim was set at a loss figure of about 2.7 million dollars.

The fire occurred in winter, and it was one of the coldest days of the year.

Due to the size of the fire, I called the local manager of the claims representatives in the area to assist me in the investigation.

We met at a restaurant to develop a strategy plan on how to attack the investigation. It was probably the most intense investigation I have ever been involved in right from the start, and on that day I had no idea that I would still be investigating it six months later.

I had ten claims representatives at my disposal, which is very unusual. Normally if I had one to assist me, I would be lucky.

I assigned a few to take the photographs, a few to draw diagrams, a few to initiate a neighborhood canvas, and others to interview the firemen who were still at the scene.

During the entire day that we worked the fire, the temperature was about five degrees with a strong wind.

Anyone who has never been to a fire scene cannot appreciate how cold it is around a building that has had water hosed on it for four to five hours. It is like being inside a freezer. Your hands don't work after about an hour, you cannot feel your feet or face, and your ears are frozen.

The scene was closed off for any person other than my adjusters. The fire department arson team was also on the scene and had been for several hours.

I was familiar with the arson investigator and had worked several fires with her before. Vicki first approached me, took me to the side, and told me that this case had to be looked at very closely because on her initial inspection, there were multiple points of origin. Multiple points of origin simply mean that the fire started in more than one place.

Normally an accidental fire starts from a short in an electrical devise, light fixture, etc. The fire spreads from that point and then catches other items in the structure on fire, and it evolves from there.

The first thing an arson investigator looks for when he inspects a fire for cause is where the most intense burning was and how quickly the fire burned.

An accidental fire starts from an electrical short or a discarded cigarette, and it takes a long time for the fire to start burning. Usually there is a large amount of smoke before the fire actually starts to flame. The fire proceeds to get hotter and hotter and eventually goes to a flashover in the room where it started. Flashover is when everything in the room is burning from ceiling to floor and wall to wall. All of the oxygen is being consumed, and there are flames everywhere. It is a very dangerous situation.

Usually when I go to a fire scene, the first thing I look for is the smoke line on the walls. When a fire starts accidentally, the smoke has a long time to deposit soot, or gray/black substance, on the walls (if the walls are still standing). The smoke line will be at least three-quarters of the distance from the ceiling to the floor, or even all the way to the floor. This means that the smoke from the fire in the room took a long time before flashover. This is an indicator of an accidental fire.

If the smoke line on the wall is high or about a quarter down from the ceiling on the wall, then I see a huge problem, because the fire burned very quickly, not allowing the smoke to fill the room before the flashover occurred. This is an indicator of a fire that was deliberately set.

I conducted a walkthrough of the fire, and I immediately saw that there were approximately six points of origin and many pour patterns on the concrete floor. Pour patterns are caused when flammable liquids are poured on the floor or on objects in the room, and the fire will burn intensely wherever the gas is poured. This leaves a pattern of the pour on the floor or the carpet in the room. This does not occur in an accidental fire.

In the office areas where the walls were still standing, the smoke line on the walls was very high, indicating a fast-burning fire.

Another factor that determined this was an arson fire was the fact that the firefighters who responded stated that the fire was burning in several areas of the large building at the same time. This would only confirm the multiple points of origin.

Whenever I discover evidence that I have a possible arson fire, the first thing I do is call in a qualified arson investigator. This is a person who has a private business and is trained in determining the cause and origin of a fire. They have to be a CFI (Certified Fire Investigator).

I had been using one CFI in the area that I completely trusted and had worked with on many fires in the past. In my business, we experience many problems involving politics. I need to tell you what happened that day.

The fire department was on the scene, and the scene was protected. They had allowed me and the claims representatives that were assisting me total access to the fire scene for our investigation, even though the arson investigators from the city were still working. We just stayed out of their way and were careful not to enter areas where they were working so as not to contaminate their scene.

I called my CFI expert to the scene, and he responded right away. When he arrived, he started his investigation, but then I was approached by the city's fire department, who said they would not allow my CFI on the scene.

This was a problem I had not experienced before. I was going to get my first taste of dirty politics that surround this job of fraud investigation. It was not that the CFI I had hired was not qualified; he was a former forensic lab manager and probably the best I had ever used. It was the fact that the city's fire department didn't want him on the scene.

It was brought to my attention that the city firefighters had a case where they stated a fire was accidental and the CFI I had hired was on the other side (insurance company). The case had gone to trial based on the findings of the CFI that the fire was arson.

During the trial, the city could not prove their accidental fire theory, and the testimony of my CFI proved to be very embarrassing for them; thus, hostility was born.

The other factor in this case is that a captain in the fire department had just retired and had started his own fire investigation business.

This line of work is very lucrative if you get an insurance company base that will hire you on a regular basis. A good fire investigator can make about $1,500 per day of investigation when you include the lab results, report, etc. If you have to go to trial on their findings, then they will have two more days of trial testimony to bill. I have seen many CFI bills that easily total five to six thousand dollars.

I think you can see where this is going.

I asked the chief why he wouldn't let my CFI on the scene. He said that they didn't trust him and they could allow whoever they wanted on a scene or prohibit anyone they chose from not going onto a fire scene.

I had to get someone on the scene right away. The findings of the fire department and my CFI's investigation had to be kept separate. Each one could form their own opinion and we could work together, but the investigations still had to be separate. We had always been told to think of this as a railroad track. Your investigations can run side by side, but they can never cross over. The bizarre fact of this theory is that the fire department can demand a complete copy of our investigation, but they *may* share information with us; they are not required to. More often than not, we give a lot but get very little in return.

The only way you can get the same amount that you give is to be cooperative and develop a rapport with all of the fire departments, police departments, state fire marshal's offices, etc.

On this case I found myself in a very bad situation. I needed my CFI to get onto the scene. I needed to develop my own evidence and have it documented, and he was being refused entry.

I made a bold move by going to the chief and asking him in a nice way, "Okay, if you won't let my CFI on the scene, who will you let in?"

The chief gave me the card of his recently retired firefighter who had started his own business.

I called him immediately, asked him if he was a CFI—he was—and if he would do the cause and origin for my company regarding this fire. He agreed and said he would be at the scene in thirty minutes.

The hardest part of this was having to fire the first CFI that I had called to the scene. The fire department stated they were having trouble removing debris from the floor, so we hired a forklift driver to come to the scene to assist in removing the debris.

If we would have not hired this driver, we would not have found the body that was at the scene. Yes, you read me right—a body. The forklift arms struck something very solid that should not have been there. The fire department carefully removed the debris in the area, and it was then discovered that the blade of the forklift had actually stuck in the head of the person who was under the debris.

It was at that point that the scene changed drastically. My crew was asked to stop their investigation and go outside of the yellow tape, which was put up immediately.

It was then that I first met the insured, the owner of the business. Let's name him Charles Smith.

I pride myself in reading people, and I immediately had a great dislike for this person. He was a fifty-year-old, heavyset guy who could be summed up as an Elvis wannabe who was in the Mafia. He had two goons with him that gave me the same impression.

I overheard the fire department asking him about the building, any possible flammables inside, and if anyone was in the building overnight. He stated that the only flammables in the building were roofing materials.

I remember having a very bad feeling at this point. The fire department was doing their investigation and I was doing mine, and we kept them separate but stayed in contact with each other. Vicki told me she would get back with me as soon as possible on the ID of the person we found at the scene and that she would share the autopsy and coroner's report with me.

Outside the building in the parking lot, we found a vehicle that had the rear hatch open, and inside were four five-gallon empty gas cans. That's a lot of gas to be spread around a building.

We finished up at the fire scene then went to speak with Charles.

We took a preliminary statement from Charles, and he said that he was home at the time of the fire. When he got the call, he came to the scene and arrived about twenty minutes later. He said that one of his employees—let's call him Nick—had been fired that day, and if the fire was arson, maybe Nick had done it. Charles also said that the truck we found with the gas cans in belonged to Nick.

Due to the weather and the late hour of the day, I advised Charles that I would contact him in a few days to get a full recorded statement from him. I relayed the information about the vehicle and its owner to Vicki. She ran a registration on the truck, and it came back to Nick. She called his house and asked if he was there. Nick's wife answered and said that he had left to go to the business but had never come home, and she was very concerned. At that point, we realized that we had found out who our forklift driver had discovered. Nick's wife confirmed that he was an employee at Charles's business and had been for ten years.

Another concern I had was that of liability. What if he had been alive when we ran the blade of the forklift through his head? We needed to find out what the cause of death was and if Nick was dead prior to our forklift driver hitting his head.

I told the new CFI to obtain samples in all of the areas where we thought an accelerant had been used and to get me a report as soon as possible. The fire department also took samples.

This is an interesting point in the investigation. Vicki, who was a single mother with two children, started getting hang-up calls that night. Also, the four five-gallon gas cans that were taken from the scene by the fire department had been put into evidence. They were to be tested for fingerprints and gas type so it could be compared to the type of accelerant that we found at the scene.

Later in the investigation, before the gas could be tested, they disappeared from the evidence room at the fire department.

I realized very early on that I was dealing with an arson fire but not a normal one; this one had complications that would eventually cause the hair to stand up on the back of my neck.

I was in my office the following day, and I received a call from the Secret Service. The agent said he could not speak over the phone but he knew that I was investigating this arson/death claim. He asked me to come to his office because he had information on Charles that I should know.

When you get a call from the Secret Service or the FBI that usually means that they want something from you. Even when I was a state trooper, the only time the FBI would cooperate with us was when they needed something. The rest of the time they would just listen but not give anything in return.

I drove to Indiana to meet with the agent. I arrived at his office not knowing what to expect. The entire drive to his office, I kept wondering if I had done anything—*are my taxes all paid. Did I declare too many gifts to the Goodwill?* I came up blank, so I went in with a clear conscience.

I was met by a middle-aged, balding agent, and let's say his name is Greg Brown. He was a nice guy, and we shot the breeze for a while, him asking me my background. When I told him I was a former state trooper and Marine and had served in Vietnam, we hit it off right away. His entire attitude changed. He had also been a Marine in Vietnam about two years after I left.

After about three cups of coffee, we finally got to the reason that I was there.

Greg asked if I was the lead investigator on the warehouse fire of the middle-aged Elvis. He also had seen the resemblance of Charles to the now-deceased King of Rock.

Greg told me that they had been watching Charles for a long time. He also said that they were getting ready to arrest Charles for a credit card scam and that there was an ongoing investigation against our insured. Greg didn't have any evidence but suspected that Charles had killed Nick. Charles was heavily in debt with Las Vegas, and Greg suspected that the fire had been started to pay off this debt.

Greg then explained Charles's credit card scam and that his opinion of Charles was not a good one. Apparently Charles was a predator who took advantage of people with bad credit and stole money from them.

Charles's scam worked like this: he would lure people to his office and have them fill out credit applications for a fee. Charles then had a dummy company that would send a letter to the applicant saying that their credit card request had been denied. The person would go back to Charles's office for a refund, only to find two very large men who would "convince" them to not pursue the issue any longer. Charles made hundreds of thousands of dollars off of this scam.

Greg told me that he could possibly help me with my fire investigation. He said that during his investigation of the credit card scam, they had done an extensive background check on Charles and discovered the huge debt he had in Vegas. Charles had a million-dollar line of credit at several casinos. Greg said Charles would usually go to Vegas two or three times per month and he had been winning, but things had changed. Charles had been on a huge losing streak for about four months, owed the casinos 2.5 million, and they wanted their money back. Greg told me that he would help me as much he could with information, but his hands were tied as far as any jurisdiction he had concerning our fire. Greg said again that there was no doubt in his mind that Charles had the fire set and had most likely killed Nick.

Greg gave me some names to start with for my investigation. The first contact was a bartender at a spot where Charles frequently hung out. I met with this guy—let's call him Ed. Ed was cooperative to a point. He said he would talk with me but would deny everything if he was ever asked and would never testify at trial. Ed knew if he did, he would be a dead man. Ed didn't like Charles, and said that was the only reason he would try to help me.

Ed said that several months before the fire, Charles was at his usual table after work with his goons. He said a large black car pulled up, and Charles became very nervous. Four large men came into the bar and approached Charles. Immediately the goons that worked for Charles walked away from him, and the four men proceeded to have a heated discussion with Charles. He said at one point Charles turned very pale.

The bartender stated that there was no doubt in his mind who these guys were other than enforcers. He said he didn't know what it was about, but after the guys left, Charles had a lengthy meeting with his goons when they were allowed to come back in.

Ed also gave me the name of a head of one of the casinos in Vegas. I called this guy—let's say his name is Al. I told Al who I was, why I was calling, and asked if he could confirm that Charles owed the casino a very large sum of money. Al said that would not be a problem. Apparently the Vegas mob is not concerned about HIPPA violations. Al checked, came back, and said that Charles owed them over a million dollars. I asked him if Charles was in any immediate danger of being snuffed or having his legs broken. Al laughed and said that was not in the future for Charles. He said yes, that used to be the way of doing things, but they were now the more gentle Vegas, and he was sure that something had been worked out with Charles to make the payment. I asked him about several men coming visit Charles in the bar shortly before a large fire at Charles's business. Would they have been from Vegas? He said that this was a good possibility. Al said they knew Charles had a large business and insurance, so the men could have suggested to him how to get our money back the casino quickly. Al said this was just speculation that this conversation never occurred, and hung up.

I knew right then that I was on thin ice, but I continued.

I later received a call from the Vicki, the fire investigator. Remember that Vicki was a single mother with two kids. She told me that she was getting very afraid because two nights in a row, there had been two men following her children home in a large, black car, and when they were in front of their house, they would just wave. Vicki also said that the hang-up calls had continued for weeks.

I told Vicki to be careful and to watch her back. I asked her if she had a chance to interview the wife of Nick, who was found dead in the building. She said she had, but the wife seemed afraid and would not really tell her anything. Vicki said they had received the autopsy back from the coroner's office and that Nick had died of blunt-force trauma to the head (not caused by the forklift) and that he had been dead before the fire had started. They knew this because he did not have any smoke in his lungs. They suspected a shovel to the back of the head. I told Vicki I would attempt an interview with the wife of Nick and get back with her.

Before I interviewed Nick's wife, I called the Secret Service to check in. The agent told me that I should start watching my back because they had heard rumors that Charles didn't like the investigation I was doing.

Greg told me that he had several informants on the street, and he had checked to see if there was a hit out on me. He said at this time there was none, but he would keep checking and again told me to watch my back.

I received a call from an employee of Charles's business. He stated that he and several of the other employees wanted to meet with me at a cabin on a nearby lake. I reluctantly agreed, because I thought the employees were going to give up the information that Charles had set the fire.

It was pitch dark when I got there. After being with them for just a few minutes, I knew it was a setup. I had pocketed a 9-mm automatic when I got out of the car, just in case. After meeting with four of the employees, it was obvious to me that there was someone else outside of the window. They started pumping me for information but were giving none. I changed my plan for this interview very quickly. They were telling me that in their opinion, Charles had set the fire and killed Nick, who was found inside, but I suspected this was a setup. The men then started asking me questions about my investigation—what I had and if I had any evidence that would put their boss in jail. The hair was standing up on the back of my neck, and the entire time, I never took my hand out of my coat pocket. My finger was on the trigger with the safety off. I told them that I didn't have any evidence to show who set the fire and I had no opinion. I told them that the employee who was killed in the fire probably set the fire himself, got caught inside, and couldn't get out. They acted like they were upset, said that was not what happened, but I knew this was an act. The person outside the window never showed himself, but again, when the hair stands up on the back of my neck, it is telling me that something is very, very wrong.

The employees met with me for one of two reasons in my opinion. They either wanted me to tell them what evidence I had—if I was too close, it is possible I would have been killed that night. The other possible reason was that they were setting me up to say things about Charles, like I thought he set the fire, before my investigation was completed. That would have been a contract bad-faith action on my part, and Charles could have sued us for a million dollars and probably won. I don't know if they knew I had the 9-mm trained on them or not, but I don't think it hurt to have never taken my hand out of my jacket. I was very careful going to my car, looking over my shoulder every second.

There were many times as a state trooper that I got this same feeling, and it always turned out very bad. If there was one thing I learned on the patrol, it was to trust my instinct, and it has always served me well in this job.

Later in the investigation, it was discovered that all of the employees there that night were involved in the setting of the fire.

I met with the wife of Nick the next day. She seemed hesitant to talk with me and said she had already talked to the police. I told her that I didn't have many questions, just a few. When I arrived, the same vehicle that Vicki had said followed her children home drove by. I obtained a registration, and it came back registered to Charles's business. I phoned it into Vicki and my boss. When I met with Nick's widow, she also had her brother present. He said that he was there to protect his sister, but also the story that they wanted to tell me needed two people instead of one.

They started by saying that her husband was a good man but he was very close with Charles and would do almost anything for him. She said that on the day of the fire, her husband came home early. The widow and her brother were at the house. Nick came in, said that he was really worried about his safety, and was afraid that Charles might try to kill him. Nick said he came home just to tell his wife this in case something happened to him. Nick said that Charles told him just a few minutes before that he had terminal cancer. Nick said that the business was in huge debt because Charles had been gambling heavily in Vegas and had lost almost all of the company's profits. Charles said that the "boys" from Vegas had paid him a visit and they told him he either burned his own building and gave Vegas the insurance money, or he would be killed. No door number two selection was offered for him at that time. Charles also told him that he had only had a few months to live. He said he wanted to burn the building down, pay off Vegas, and then his daughter would have his life-insurance policy to live on, plus anything that was left over from the insurance money after paying off Vegas.

Nick had told his wife that an employee of Charles was with him when they said this. He was Charles's right-hand man, and his name was Joe. Charles asked Nick to burn the building for him. He said he needed to be away when it happened and have plenty of witnesses around so he would have an alibi.

Nick said that he just couldn't do it; he knew something would go wrong and he would go to jail. The insured asked him several times to do it and then offered him $10,000 to do the job.

Nick told his wife that he told Charles he needed to go home and think about it. Nick was told to be back at the business in one hour and to not tell anyone about the offer made to him.

Nick told his wife and his brother-in-law the entire story. Nick said he was afraid to go back to the business, because he knew they would kill him, but he didn't want to not show up, for fear they would come to his house and possibly kill his wife as well. The brother was very helpful in the fact that number one, he overheard the entire conversation, and number two, the brother went with Nick out to his truck and could confirm that he looked in the back of his truck and there were no gas cans. The wife said Nick didn't even own any gas cans. She said that was the last time she spoke with her husband, and the next thing she knew, she heard the fire trucks. She went to the business (which was only four blocks away from her home), and there she saw her husband's truck parked up against the front doors of the building. She said that the time lapse between the offer and the fire trucks coming to the neighborhood was about one hour. I knew from that statement that I could put the insured, Charles, at the scene of the fire less than one hour before it started.

She didn't say anything to the fire department that night or when they contacted her for a statement two days after the fire. She said it was two to three days after the fire when she was told that they had identified her husband as the one who was found dead inside the building. She was also told that the fire department thought he was a disgruntled employee and that he had set fire to the building but cornered himself, could not escape, and got killed by the smoke and fire. Nick's wife was also informed that Charles made a statement to the police that Nick had threatened to burn down the building earlier that day because he was upset about not getting a pay raise or bonus.

I asked the widow if she and her brother would be willing to testify to what they had told me, and they said they would.

My idea was that if I could get enough evidence against Charles, coupled with the widow and brother's statements added to it, we could possibly go under the dying declaration doctrine. This doctrine is when someone makes a statement that is considered to be the truth because he is just about to meet his maker.

The employee made this statement about forty-five minutes before his time of death.

I started digging into the investigation that would take the better part of six months of my career.

Nick's truck was identified, and the gas cans that were found in the back were considered to be his by the police and fire department. They thought they had an open-and-shut case, but Vicki disagreed. She said she wanted to investigate it further, but she was starting to become afraid for herself and her family.

Vicki said she had received a call from a former employee of Charles who wanted to speak to me. Let's call this guy Tom. Tom wanted to meet with me at a restaurant in the area. I set it up and met with him. He said he thought I should know about something that happened about a month before the fire. He received a call from Charles, who wanted him to meet him on a deserted road just outside of the city. When he met Charles, he was shown a gun and several thousand dollars in his wallet. He told Tom that he had cancer, didn't want to go through all of the sickness and treatments, and had purchased several insurance policies for his daughter. Charles said that he didn't think the policies would pay for a suicide, so he told Tom that if he shot him, then it would look like it was a robbery and he could have the money. Tom told Charles that he was crazy and walked away. The next week he was fired.

This prompted me to contact the local police, and they immediately shut down the credit card company that Charles was operating. The Secret Service charged him with several crimes related to the scam. Charles ended up paying a huge fine and received two years probation.

I started looking around the area to see if Charles's alibi during the fire could be broken. In questioning Charles, he said he was at a restaurant with his right-hand man, his girlfriend, several waitresses, and the bartender could verify that he was there at the time of the fire.

I knew this was a lie, so I started asking at several gas stations to see if anyone had any videotapes of someone buying gas in a can on the night of the fire. By doing this, I came up with a tape of a vehicle that looked like one owned by Charles's business. The video, however, did not show the face of the person buying the gas or the license plate of the vehicle. I tried to track the purchase time back to the cash register receipts, but the person had paid cash (not good for me).

I also attempted to interview several drive-thru liquor stores close to the fire scene. The second one I went to knew Charles. I had photos of Charles printed up so I could show them to anyone who may have information. I showed an employee the photo of Charles, and the employee said he was positive that Charles stopped in for cigarettes and beer the night of the fire, shortly before he heard the fire trucks.

This would be extremely important evidence for me, because Charles was supposedly twenty-five minutes away at a restaurant on the night of the fire then went home and received the call from his foreman that the building was on fire. This call was reportedly made from the employee's cell phone.

The drive-thru employee researched his sales slips, and even though he didn't have a video of the vehicle with Charles in it, he described Charles's vehicle and Charles's goon with him at the time of the purchase. The employee said they bought a pack of Marlboros and a six pack of Bud. The receipt showed that the purchase had been made just before the fire was called in. I took the receipt to Vicki immediately.

Vicki stated that she didn't think the statement of the drive-thru employee and the receipt was worth very much, because we could not tie the receipt to Charles other than with the employee's testimony. Any good attorney could tear it apart on the stand. I disagreed with her and told her I thought the evidence was strong.

Vicki said that they took prints off of the gas cans found at the scene in Nick's truck, she ran them but didn't get a match. She said that she would file away the prints in case we ever got a possible suspect that we would have prints on to compare them.

Vicki also stated that the gas cans were now missing in the property room at the fire department. She was getting worried that someone at the fire department was helping Charles, and she didn't know who to trust. She said that suspicious cars were driving up and down her street, driving by very slowly, and just staring at her and her children. This was getting to be an everyday occurrence, and the hang-up calls were getting worse. She said that she was going to have the phone company tap her phone to see where the calls were coming from. As soon as Vicki put the tap on her phone, the calls stopped. Coincidence? I think not.

I thought the evidence of the receipt along with the drive-thru employee's testimony was huge. What I didn't know was the parameters of what the prosecutor would take or not take in the county we were working in. Vicki was actually trying to do something with this murder/arson, but her hands were tied. She told me that for a conviction of arson in her county, you better have a videotape of the arsonist at the scene with the lit match in his hand.

All of the reports from the new CFI started coming in, and it was confirmed that we had a poured-gasoline fire with about four points of origin as evidence. The grade of gasoline in the cans that was left matched the grade of gas that was found at the scene.

My circumstantial evidence was starting to build. The next documents I asked for were cell phone records and home phone records for the foreman and Charles. We have a database system that can check to see what tower a cell phone call was made from. I was able to show that by the statement the foreman gave me and what he did that night was a lie. The truth was that he was sitting on an overpass very close to the business when the fire was started and called Charles as soon as he heard the first fire truck.

It was also funny that there was no way to prove that Charles was home at the time the call came in. Someone answered the phone at his house, and the foreman said he spoke with Charles, but this could not be verified.

Later, Charles's girlfriend would testify that Charles was home at the time and that he answered the phone.

This did not jive with the drive-thru employee, who swore that Charles was sitting in his drive-thru one block away from the fire scene when the fire trucks were responding.

The next thing was the restaurant employees. I interviewed six of them, and three stated that they were sure Charles was there all night until just before the fire occurred, when he left to go home. The other three would not lie for Charles, and they actually said that Charles had left hours before the fire and had not returned.

The bartender also confirmed that Charles had left several hours before the fire, and he said Charles only lived a few blocks from the restaurant.

I asked for sales receipts for the restaurant that night, and we were able to show that Charles did in fact sign a credit card receipt two hours before the fire alarm went off.

I took all of this to Vicki, and she again stated that Charles could have gone back into the restaurant and paid cash for more drinks. I had three employees testifying against each other, and the prosecutor would not take the case.

I asked Charles to come in for a full recorded interview, and he showed up with his attorney, which is very unusual.

I have interviewed a lot of people in my career. Many have been murderers, thieves, child molesters, burglars, auto thieves, professional auto accident rings, the Vietnamese Mafia, the Russian Mafia, and American Mafia. Charles, in my opinion, was just pure evil. I asked Charles where he was on the night of the fire and who he was with. I also ask him if he returned to the business anytime that night. I also asked him if he saw Nick that night before the fire after they left for work, etc.

Charles denied ever going back to the business after closing at five o'clock. He said he went to the restaurant for dinner and drinks, and when he left, he went straight home and didn't leave until he got the phone call about the fire. I asked him if he set the fire or if he hired someone to set the fire, and he said no. I could not get any more accusatory at that point, because I was still investigating the claim and had no clear facts yet. I asked Charles if he was ill, and he said no. I asked him if he had any financial problems, and he said, "None that have not been taken care of." He said that I could check his books and I could clearly see that he had a profitable business. In fact, this was probably the only true statement he made to me. His business did in fact turn out to be profitable. The only problem was that he had been spending all of the profit gambling in Vegas. I asked him about Vegas, and he said he had an open line of credit there for a million dollars and had been winning, not losing.

I told Charles and his attorney that I was finished asking my questions, and at that point Charles just leaned across the table and smiled at me. Not a "hey, I like you" smile, but an "I know you know, and you know I know, now prove it" smile. I told Charles and his attorney that I would be calling them in for an examination under oath within the next few weeks.

I made a timeline driving to and from Charles's home to the business four times. In the timeline, I averaged the time it took to drive from Charles's home to the business during the four drives. I went through the cell phone records and found the time that Charles supposedly received the call from his foreman. Charles had ample time to get the call, get his coat on, go to his car, etc. I calculated the time it should have taken Charles to get to the business. I had the time of his arrival based on interviews with firemen at the scene and a radio dispatch stating that the insured had just arrived on the scene. The timeline and the actual time it should have taken Charles to get to the business did not match up. There was no way Charles could have driven from his home to the business, based on the time study, and he got there way too quickly. My theory was that he was sitting down the street from the fire scene, waited on the fire trucks, and then shortly after that arrived on the scene. He was probably sitting there drinking his six pack, smoking his Marlboros.

We did an examination under oath, and Charles lied about everything, saying he did not start the fire and had nothing to do with the murder.

We then had to consider all of the evidence we had. It was not the strongest case I ever had, and none of the other restaurant employees would testify against Charles, because they were afraid of him. I had a timeline, but it could possibly be defeated at trial because of not being able to actually prove Charles was at the drive-thru except for the drive-thru employee's testimony, and everything else was circumstantial. I knew that Vegas would not come and testify or any of Charles' employees that were loyal to him.

I did have an ace in the hole. The ace was Nick's wife and her brother, who said they would testify even after they had been threatened over the phone not to. I figured that if I could get in their statements and the judge would allow them to testify with the dying declaration rule, we could win this case in front of a jury and possibly even see criminal charges filed against Charles.

We denied the claim. Naturally, Charles's attorney immediately filed suit against us for the amount of the claim and a million dollars in bad faith.

The next course of action was depositions prior to the trial. I will never forget sitting across from Charles and his attorney. When I was asked who I thought set the fire, I was finally allowed to give my opinion. I said, pointing to Charles, "He did, and there is no doubt in my mind that he killed Nick!"

I will also never forget the smile that came across Charles' mouth. The devil smiled, and then he just laughed.

Our attorneys filed for summary judgment using the theory of dying declaration, and that is when it happened. The judge denied our summary judgment and stated he would not allow any testimony from the wife of Nick or her brother at the trial. He said that he had researched the dying declaration, and the statement has to be uttered when the person is actually dying and not before the death was imminent.

At that time our attorneys did not want to go to trial, and a compromised settlement was made with Charles and his attorney. It was for a smaller percentage of the claim, and they dropped the bad-faith action.

To this day this case still bothers me. I think about Charles often. I heard from Vicki not very long ago. She said she still has the prints from the gas can and she runs them once a year. She and I both agreed that someday, the prints may be identified. If we do identify them, possibly the person will testify against Charles and we can finally bring someone to justice. The last I heard Charles is still alive and his cancer did not take him from this earth yet.

THE ONE THAT GOT AWAY

This next case made me actually respect the insured, because he literally pulled one over on me and got away with a very large claim.

The amazing thing is that I did my job well, proved that the claim was a false one, and the insured should have been arrested for insurance fraud. This was never going to happen, at least not in this lifetime.

The only reason I had any respect for this person was because of professional courtesy. The insured had his back against the wall and needed some money to tie him over until he was back in good graces with the "family." Yes, I am talking about *the family*, or the Mafia. I am going to call this guy Tony Capriole—that is as far as I will go with the name or even where this took place. Tony was one of the most colorful and coolest characters that I have ever come across. I actually grew to like this guy and his wife.

Tony was high up in "the family" but had really messed up in Vegas, where he was the manager of a casino. The family decided to punish him and send him to a Podunk town where his father-in-law had a very good business, let's say, selling widgets.

The father-in-law was a very wealthy man, or at least he was until Tony took him for a bundle.

Tony married the widget maker's daughter, who was a very striking lady, and they had a son.

The deal was that Tony worked in this town close to his father-in-law, where coincidentally the Mafia had a money-laundering operation going on. Tony's job was to work at this operation for two years, and if he did okay there "paying his dues," so to speak, he would be given the hotel to manage in, let's say, New York.

Tony had been told that if he did well with the money laundering and the hotel in New York, that he would eventually get back to Vegas and run his own casino. My story starts in this Podunk town in a southern city.

I was really close friends with a claims representative in this southern state. We will call him Bob. Bob called me in my office on a Friday morning and said, "You are not going to believe this one!"

I asked him what he had, and he gave me the background on Tony and his father-in-law. Tony, his wife, and son had been out in the Gulf of Mexico fishing, and his $50,000 Rolex watch had dropped off of his wrist into the ocean. I told Bob that I would be down on Monday, but I wanted to know when this had occurred. He said that Tony had supposedly lost the watch on Saturday but didn't tell the captain of the boat about it until they were back at shore. Tony had not called his agent until the next Friday morning, nearly a week later.

I know you are not all insurance investigators, but don't several things come to mind that might not be right with this story so far?

First, who would wear a $50,000 Rolex watch on a fishing boat in the Gulf of Mexico? I know you are thinking, maybe a Mafia guy, but I don't think I would.

Second, if I did have one on and I lost it, I would probably tell the captain, "Oh, crap, my $50,000 Rolex watch just dropped off the side of the boat into the ocean!" Maybe the captain is a diver? Maybe we are not in that deep of water? Maybe the captain could have marked the latitude and longitude where it occurred and divers could come back later and try to retrieve the watch?

Third, if you would have lost your $50,000 Rolex watch in the Gulf of Mexico on a Saturday afternoon about two o'clock and your agent was in a close southern state, what would you do as soon as you got to shore? Or better yet, if you had a cell phone, who would you call? I probably would call my insurance agent to make sure that it is covered and that the loss is reported and find out how I submit the claim.

Most people who insure jewelry do so because they feel as though they have to. If they have a good agent, they will take the time to explain to the insured that if they have any jewelry valued at over $2,500, they need to insure it specifically. If they choose not to buy separate insurance for the jewelry, their total jewelry loss will be covered for the amount of $2,500 for theft and fire. It will not be covered for just losing the item. If you pay the expensive premium for a jewelry floater, then the item is covered for whatever the item is appraised for, no matter what happened to it.

In my opinion, this is the insurance industry's biggest mistake of writing lost jewelry and it gives many of their insured's a license to steal from them, and it is very hard to prove.

If you wake up one morning and the $100,000 bracelet that you put on your nightstand before you went to sleep is now gone and there had been no forced entry into your home, the insurance company will have to pay you $100,000 unless they can prove fraud.

In Tony's case, several things went into the "red flag" bin when I looked at the file.

First, Tony had been riding on the coattails, so to speak, of his wealthy father-in-law. The father-in-law employed the majority of the people in the small southern town where they lived. Tony had married the wealthy businessman's daughter after he had wooed her on a Vegas vacation. Tony's wife was a very beautiful woman. There is no doubt in my mind that they really loved each other. They had one son together; he was their world. When Tony was asked to leave Vegas, I'm sure the family chose the small southern town because it was close to his wife's family. Whatever the case was, they ended up close to the father-in-law's home, and the insurance coverage for Tony was written through the same agent as the father-in-law. The red flag on the coverage was that the appraisal for the watch had been written about four months prior to the policy being issued. The watch was supposedly purchased in Las Vegas about one year prior to the policy being written. Why wasn't the watch insured before? Why was the appraisal written just before the watch was insured? Normally if someone buys a $50,000 Rolex watch, they get an appraisal and then insure it; this didn't happen in this case.

The second red flag that I saw was when I met with Tony for the first time. He had a videotape for me of his son, his wife, and himself on the boat, and three times the video had him holding up his wrist so the camera could see the watch. It was obviously a staged videotape. Of course, the tape did not show him fishing and the watch falling off in the Gulf of Mexico, as he had claimed. It is very rare that an insured has a tape to prove that something existed that they are making a claim for.

The third red flag was after I initially spoke with Tony (no recorded statement yet). He gave me the name of the fishing boat and the name of the captain he had hired the day they went out. I called the captain, and this was the first of several mistakes that Tony made. The captain remembered taking Tony and his family out on a charter, but he said he didn't remember any Rolex watch being worn or lost into the ocean. The captain said that Tony never said anything to him or the first mate when he got off of the boat. He also made the comment, "I would have noticed a $50,000 Rolex if he had been wearing it and, "Who in their right mind would wear such an expensive watch when they were fishing?"

The captain said he would check with the booking agency he used to see if Tony had mentioned anything to them. He discovered that Tony had called the booking agency the next day and said, "If you get a call from an insurance company, I just wanted to let you know that I dropped my watch off the side of the boat while I was fishing."

The booking agent said to me on the phone, "I don't want to tell you how to do your job, but if you would have lost a $50,000 watch in the ocean, wouldn't you have told the captain when it happened, or at least told them about it when you got to the dock?" and I completely agreed.

The fourth red flag was enormous. I wanted to get as much investigated and as many people contacted as possible before I met with Tony for a statement. I do this so that I am physically and mentally prepared to understand as much about the case as I can, so the interview can be a successful one. I went to the local police department to see what they might know about Tony. Wow, did I get an earful. They proceeded to tell me about his ties to the Mafia, which were well known. They also told me that his father-in-law, who was a good friend of the police department, hated Tony and had recently gotten into a huge argument with him. The argument was because the father-in-law found out about his Mafia ties, and this upset him. The father-in-law had also given Tony a loan that had not been paid back. The father-in-law went to the daughter and told her she needed to leave Tony and move back home with his grandchild because he was afraid of the lifestyle that she would be subjected to.

Well, as you can guess—and this happens many times when a parent tries to intervene in a marriage problem—it backfired. The daughter was very much in love with Tony, and she knew about his Mafia ties before she married him. She went directly to Tony and told him what her father had wanted her to do. Tony went to the father-in-law's house, threatened him, and told him to stay out of his personal life if he knew what was good for him.

Shortly after that, the police department discovered that there was a hit put out on the father-in-law.

The police chief had ties with a former Secret Service agent who had a protection business. This agent was called in, and for the last three months, the former agent and four of his men were protecting the father-in-law 24/7. They would take him to work, guard his house at night, and go everywhere with him. I was also told that all of these men were armed, had licenses to carry weapons, and were very competent. They had told the police that there was no doubt in their minds that there were men in town to take out the father-in-law and their presence was the only thing that stopped this from happening. The police told me that I needed to speak with the father-in-law before I did anything.

When I left the police department, I thought to myself, *Just what have you gotten yourself into this time, Jack?* Many times, police are very leery to discuss any of their cases with an outsider.

I always try to have Ohio State Highway Patrol patches to trade for information with cops, but in this case they were more than willing to give me the information. I still think that the police detective I spoke with was getting a kickback from the father-in-law for setting up the protection, or he was getting one from the Secret Service agent for calling him in for the job, but could never prove anything.

I called the father-in-law, and he agreed to meet with me at his workplace. When I arrived (at the widget company), I was very impressed. When I saw the size of the building, the number of workers (probably 150), and the plush office of the father-in-law, I knew right away that this guy had some major bucks. I found out later that he was a multimillionaire. He was a pretty nice guy, but I knew that if it had not been for this investigation, he wouldn't have given me the time of day. He was a very busy man, and I could tell that his time was very valuable to him. He proceeded to tell me the same story as the police and that he was afraid for his life, his wife's life, and that of his daughter and grandchild. He said that he had been told by Tony if he ever interfered in his life again in any way that he would never see his daughter or grandchild again.

The father-in-law said that his daughter and grandchild would still come to his house and visit, but Tony would not come, and they were not on speaking terms at all. He confirmed that the former Secret Service agents were still following him everywhere he went. He asked me what type of claim Tony had filed with us. I told him that it was for a $50,000 Rolex watch that he had lost in the ocean in the Gulf of Mexico. He started laughing. He said that the watch did exist but it didn't even belong to Tony. He said that a business partner of Tony's in Vegas owed Tony about $40,000, and Tony was just holding the watch until the debt was paid. He even gave me the guy's name, and he had a photo of the guy—let's call this guy Sam. Sam was a personal friend of Tony's and was single; he was very close to Tony and his wife and loved their child. He would always be there for holidays and birthdays.

The farther-in-law said that he was concerned about his grandson being around Sam, so he had the former Secret Service guy check him out. Sam was believed to be a strong arm for the Mafia, and his reputation of being feared in the Vegas area followed him around. He gave me Sam's name and phone number.

After meeting with the police and the father-in-law, I called Tony and scheduled to meet with him to take a recorded statement.

When I met with him at his house, he was very friendly and cordial. He was Italian and had coal-black hair. He reminded me of a former Mafia lieutenant that I met at an insurance meeting, named Michael Franzese. Michael had come to a national SIU meeting to speak with us about how he defrauded insurance companies for years and made millions for "the family" in black-market gasoline. Tony and Michael were both very nice guys, and I really liked them a lot, but I am sure both had backgrounds that would make the normal Joe on the street wet his pants. Michael wrote a book called *Blood Covenant* about how he broke away from the Mafia and lived to tell about it. I would highly recommend this book to anyone, and it is enjoyable reading. I don't know why, but I have a knack of getting along with most criminals. I think it is just my good looks. Ha!

Back to Tony. I got to meet his wife, and, as I said before, she was strikingly beautiful and also friendly to me. I started the interview, asked how the loss occurred, and Tony stated that he had the Rolex watch on his wrist and had been having trouble with the clasp. He knew it was stupid that he didn't get it fixed, but he just had not gotten around to it.

I asked him his background, and he said that he had a casino in Vegas. Then he came to where he was now to run a company for his family, and if he did well there, he would next get a hotel in New York then eventually go back to Vegas.

This is the same story I had been told by the police.

I asked him about when he purchased the watch, and he showed me an appraisal that was from a jewelry store in Vegas. The appraisal was only three months old, and that was about the same time that Tony had been sent to this southern town and taken out a policy on the coattails of his father-in-law. The watch had been scheduled for $50,000 at the same time on the new policy. The appraisal had a name and phone number on it, which became very valuable to me later on.

Tony then said that he was catching a fish, his hands got wet, and eventually his wrist, and all of a sudden the watch came loose and slipped off of his wrist and dropped into the ocean. He asked if I had watched the videotape that his wife had shot on the boat, showing that he indeed had the watch on that day. I commented that the video did show that he had a watch on of some type, but I couldn't tell by the video if it was a Rolex. How did I know that it was the same Rolex that he had scheduled?

He laughed at this statement and he said, "Can you prove that it wasn't?"

One part of my interviewing technique that I have discussed before is the summary of the statement given by any insured or claimant. I have them tell me the story, and then I repeat the story to them and see if they will agree and commit to everything they have said. Then I ask them if the story is true. If they say yes, then I always ask them, "Why should I believe what you have told me?"

The normal answer should be, "Because it is the truth," or, "I have told the truth!"

It is a very simple statement to make, and a truthful person will always answer with one of these statements. The guilty person or the person who is committing a fraud or lying to you will say everything but, "Because it is the truth!" I have had people start talking, filling up two transcribed pages explaining to me why I should believe them, and all they had to do was say, "Because it is the truth!"

This is the KDI I refer to as a "question with a question" and it is one of the best deception technique answers that I see. When someone answers a question I ask with a question, they are lying. I have never had this fail in any investigation. I asked Tony this question and his answer was, "Why shouldn't you?"

Right then I knew I had a problem. Now, I know you are thinking, *Okay, you know that he is lying, and you are so confident about this—why didn't you just at that point say to Tony, "Hey, I know you are lying. Fess up"?* Well, it's not that easy. A polygraph test, a voice stress analysis, and any other deception tests such as my KDIs are not admissible in court. It is an investigative tool. When someone tells me the truth about 75 percent of the claim and then only lies to me about 25 percent, then this saves me time. I only have to verify the 25 percent of their story.

I never let the person that I am interviewing know that I have just run my own "verbal polygraph," so to speak, on them. This would come back and haunt me on the stand at trial if I had to explain what I used, why I used it, and if I was an expert in this. I only use the information to help me with the investigation, and everything after that has to be good, physical evidence that I can take to trial.

I asked Tony if the watch was his, and he said it was. I asked him if it belonged to Sam, and he got his really confused look on his face.

Tony never asked me how I knew that; he just cocked his head to the side and said, "You are really good!"

He said that the watch used to belong to Sam, but Sam owed him some money and gave it to him. Tony also said that he had the watch scheduled after he got it from Sam. He then added, with a smile on his face, that you never know when you might drop a watch in the ocean and need insurance on it!

I told Tony that I would finish my investigation and get back with him as soon as possible. He said, "Tell you what, if you pay me today, I will take $35,000 and save your company $15,000. That's all I need to get me by for a while." I told him I didn't settle claims—all I did was investigate them—but I would pass that offer over to the claims adjuster.

I left the house and drove by the money-laundering fake business that Tony reportedly ran. It was about two o'clock in the afternoon. There were no lights on, no employees inside, and I saw no inventory. I checked with the police again about the business, and they stated that they knew that the business was a front for Mafia money laundering.

They said that Tony was very well protected and they could not get enough of anything he had done wrong to charge him. The father-in-law had refused to file charges for criminal threats, so their hands were tied.

I contacted Sam about one week later, and Sam verified that he had given the watch to Tony because he owed him money. I asked Sam where he originally got the watch. He said, "I got it at a pawn shop here in Vegas." I asked him if he had a receipt. He said no. I asked him if he knew the name of the pawn shop, and he said no. I asked him how he paid for the watch, and while he was laughing over the phone (he was in Vegas), he said, "Cash, of course!" I asked him where he got the cash, and he said he usually carried ten to twenty thousand dollars with him and he had the cash at his house to pay for the watch.

I asked him what he did for a living, and he said, "I am a problem solver."

I did not even bother to elaborate on that statement.

I asked him if Tony had told him about losing the watch, and he said he had. He said Tony lost it while out fishing. He said that was really too bad because he was going to buy the watch back from Tony because he had come into some money. I asked him if Tony had told him what to say, and he said he had not.

I called the jeweler in Vegas about one week later. I had heard prior to calling the jeweler that Tony had moved to New York and was living on one of the top floors at the hotel he was managing.

I asked the jeweler if he knew Tony and Sam. He said that he was very familiar with them and that they did business with him all of the time. I asked him if he sold the watch to Sam or Tony, and he said he had not. The jeweler said that he was asked to repair the watch and he was waiting on parts. He said that he was also asked several weeks before to write an appraisal on the watch and send it to Tony in the southern state. He said that Tony had called him and asked him for the appraisal, and it was well known that Tony and Sam were in the Mafia, so he asked no questions. He said that Tony had spent a lot of money in his jewelry store, mainly on women's jewelry.

I told the jeweler about the watch slipping off Tony's wrist and falling into the ocean. He just laughed. I had given him the serial number of the watch, and he said, "Your claim is impossible, because when Tony said he lost the watch in Florida, it was in my shop for repair." He said he was sure of it. He still had the watch and he was waiting for parts. He checked the serial number, and it was the same. I recorded the statement with the jeweler. I was baffled at this point that Tony had thought I would not check out the appraisal and actually call and talk to the jeweler. Later, I discovered why he was not concerned in the least. I asked the jeweler if he would be willing to testify, and he said yes. He said he hated to see insurance companies ripped off for fraudulent claims and he ran a legitimate business.

I then called Rolex to verify the serial number for the watch and to see if they could track the owner. The serial number did match, but they said that the watch had changed hands several times and they had lost track of it.

With this new evidence, I thought I had just busted this case wide open. I was feeling very cocky and called Tony in New York. I told him I was getting on the next plane and I could meet with him later that day. Tony was also feeling cocky and said, "Come on up. I'll have the coffee on."

I got off the plane and drove to the hotel. I went to the front desk and asked for Tony. At that point a very well-dressed goon who obviously had on a shoulder hostler under his suit came over. He was six feet five inches tall and weighed about three hundred pounds. He asked what I wanted with Tony. I told him I had an appointment. He made a quick call and then said to follow him. We rode the elevator up to the top floor, and when I was ushered in, I could not believe what I saw. The room that Tony and his family lived in was an entire floor of the hotel. It had two bedrooms, four baths, and a huge living room with a fireplace right in the middle. Tony met me at the door and was very cordial. His wife was also there with their son. He asked her to leave the room, and she did immediately.

He then said, "What's up? Did you bring my check?"

I told him that I had a problem with his claim and cautioned him about taking the claim any further because of insurance fraud and the possible penalties of what he had done.

He said, "I don't know what you are talking about," and that he still wished to pursue his claim, but now it was for the full $50,000.

I smiled and said, "Don't say I didn't give you a chance," and then I pulled out the recorder and pushed play. The jeweler's voice came on. He identified himself and his business and stated the watch was in his possession the entire time that this loss was supposed to have occurred. He then he went on to say that he still had the watch in his shop. The jeweler also stated he knew the insured and he would testify against him.

Tony just smiled, and then he sort of laughed. He said, "You came all the way to New York with just this?"

I said yes and confidently gave him one last chance to withdraw his claim before I would be forced to go to the authorities. Tony asked me if I would mind waiting a minute because he had to make a phone call. He came back into the room and asked if I still had the same cell phone number.

I said I did.

He said, "Would you like a cup of coffee? You will be getting a call in about twenty minutes." I said I would, still thinking I had won this one and thinking that maybe his attorney was going to call me, asking for some type of deal. In about twenty minutes my cell phone rang, and it was the jeweler. This is what he said: "Mr. Morgan, this is Mr. Smith from the jewelry store in Vegas." I recognized his voice, but it seemed to be shaking. "I just had two very large gentlemen in suits come into my store, and one is on each side of me right now. I just wanted to say that they have told me that I do not have the watch in my store, I have never had the watch in my store for any length of time, and all I did was write an appraisal on it. I was mistaken when I told you that it was, and this is my story that I will be sticking to. I will never testify in court. Do you understand what I am telling you?"

I told him, "Yes, I understand everything now."

I hung up the phone and looked at Tony. I said, "I have been doing this for many years and have very seldom been beaten on a claim, but I have to admit, you are really good."

Tony just smiled and said, "Do you want another cup of coffee?"

I said, "No. I probably should be leaving."

He said, "Stay in touch. I will be waiting on my check." The goon then escorted me outside to my rental car, and I left.

The claim was paid for $50,000, and I never heard from Tony again.

I pride myself in my investigations. When I tell the company that I work for that we can win a case at trial after a denial, I mean it. I have only lost one trial in thirty-four years of my career as a Special Investigator. Tony was clever, he got away with insurance fraud, and there was nothing I could do about it. Tony, my hat's off to you.

JUSTIFIABLE HOMICIDE OR MURDER?

During the investigation of this next case, I came the closest I have ever come to getting myself killed, yet is my favorite story to date. I am not going to express my opinion as to what really happened concerning the final outcome. I am simply going to give you the facts of the case that I developed during my investigation. I want you, the reader, to be the judge and the jury.

I had a good friend with me during the end of this investigation, and due to the still very serious nature of the investigation, I am going to only use is nickname. He was new to my SIU unit, and I was breaking him in at the time.

In our unit we have some unique characters, and their nicknames describe how we feel about them or are directly assigned to something about their personality or something they have done in the past or not done.

Let's start with the boss. His nickname is Dutch Boy because he was raised in a strict Pennsylvania Dutch background. There is Cobra (who likes to think of himself as having the linguistic tongue of a snake), Idle Time (whom we kid about not having enough work to do), and the Big Bopper (who is always singing tunes from the sixties and knows all of the songs, words, and artists). Others are simple, such as Z-man, Sky, (helicopter pilot), Greenie, etc. The good friend who was with me at the last part of this investigation was Joe Momma; his partner is called Tonto. Others are Jimmy V, Bones, Hackman, Hag, Ant-ney, and about ten others that I will not bore you with, and that is all I am going to say about that.

I will not mention any states or counties, but several years ago there were corrupt sheriffs down south, and they had total control over everything that happened in their county. The FBI was afraid to even go into their counties to do an investigation because they didn't know if they would leave alive or not.

I have been escorted out of these counties by corrupt police. I have had my entire file that I shared with a law enforcement officer given to the other side's attorney, and I have even been told, "Leave this county now," and "I never want to see you back here again." The reason for this is because I was investigating a friend or relative of theirs and they had the power to stop my investigation by just making me leave. I consider myself a brave person, and I will not back down from almost anything (heights and snakes excluded). Remember, I was a Marine Corps infantryman was in combat for eleven months and got hit on two different occasions in some very bad battles. However, I am not stupid, and when in a situation where the outcome is not in my favor, I choose the battle that lets me live to fight another day.

This case was referred to me by one of our claims representatives after an optometrist's office we insured had burned to the ground. The fire department believed the fire to be arson. The fire reportedly had many points of origin, and an accidental fire had been ruled out completely.

The office had been forcibly entered, and it appeared that the origin of the fire was targeted toward a file room, where many file cabinets were located, as well as the office of the owner.

We insured the business and the building that the business was located in.

I went to the scene immediately, as I try to do with any fire. I was in the area the next morning after the fire. The building appeared as though it had several gallons of some type of accelerant poured on it, and it smelled like kerosene. When I spoke with the fire department, they told me that whoever set the fire had left a gallon of kerosene at the scene and it had a specific brand name on it.

I met with our policy holder; let's call him Dr. Dan. Although he appeared to be not telling me everything, I ruled him out as the one that set the fire. He had an ironclad alibi. Now, does this mean he didn't hire someone to set the fire? This remained to be seen.

I had a very good contact in the area of the fire at the local sheriff's department. I had worked with him before, and we had a very good working relationship. When I told him about this one, he became very interested, dropped what he was doing, and we immediately started the investigation.

Whenever the arsonist leaves something at the scene, especially a gas can or a kerosene container, the best thing to do is canvas the neighborhood.

This will only work if you get on the fire investigation right away. That is because the goal of the neighborhood canvas is to check with every convenience store, mom-and-pop store, or gas station in the area to see if they have a video camera. If they don't, check whether or not they remembered someone buying a large amount of kerosene, gasoline, or whatever was used to set the fire. We knew what brand of kerosene the arsonist used, and we were trying to find a convenience store that sold this brand.

We split up the area, and after interviewing about seven convenience stores, I hit a goldmine. This convenience store sold that brand of kerosene, and they remembered a guy who came in early in the morning, about one o'clock. He was a white male about thirty-five years old, and he bought several gallons of kerosene, a lighter and lighter fluid. They even had a good-quality videotape of the purchase he made, including audio.

The best thing about this video was the fact that our fire had started about thirty minutes after the purchase and was only about a mile from the convenience store where the purchase was made.

I called the sheriff's detective and told him what I had. He immediately came over with a subpoena he had obtained for a copy of the video.

When the detective from the sheriff's department arrived, we viewed the videotape.

It showed the subject coming in and picking up three gallons of kerosene in plastic containers and paying for them. He then went back outside. After a few minutes, he came back in, bought three more gallons, and at the register said, "Do you sell lighter fluid and lighters?"

They said they did, and he purchased both items, including the additional three gallons of kerosene.

He paid cash. In the video you could see the subject go outside to a car, but the vehicle was obscured by a display in the store, and you could not see anyone else in the car or the license plate. This is very important for you to remember later.

The detective, after viewing the tape, stated, "I know this guy!" He said that he had been in trouble before but he wasn't that bad of a guy. The detective said he knew where he lived.

We drove to the subject's home. He gave us no trouble and was taken into custody for questioning.

At the sheriff's office, he broke down and gave us an unbelievable story that would prove to be his own doom.

Let's call this guy George.

George stated that he had a girlfriend named Wanda. He said that he and Wanda had been dating for several months and it was getting serious, but she eventually told him of a problem she had, and it needed to be resolved before their relationship could go any further. I can understand why George eventually gave in to the plan, because Wanda was a very attractive woman.

Wanda told him that at her last job, at the optometrist's office, she had had an affair with her boss, the eye doctor, and eventually asked him for a loan. The amount was $20,000, and she signed an IOU. She said that the relationship went bad and eventually, because the eye doctor was afraid his wife would discover what happened, he fired Wanda. He not only fired her but told her she only had six months to pay back the signed note.

Wanda came from an influential family in another state where her father was a huge supporter of the current sheriff, in the financial way, if you get my drift.

The place where the fire occurred was only about fifty miles from where Wanda lived, even though it was in another state.

The county where she resided was right against the state line. George also lived in the same county. Wanda told George that she could not pay back the money and didn't want her family to know what she did. She only wanted to make the IOU go away. She also wanted to ruin the eye doctor's business and destroy his building out of just pure hatred.

Wanda asked George to help her break into the optometrist's office and burn the area where she knew her old boss kept the IOU, in a file cabinet she knew was locked.

He said that he agreed to help her and they left for the office building. George first stopped at the convenient store and bought three gallons of kerosene. When he went back to the car where Wanda was waiting, she became very upset with him and said, "That's not enough, you idiot. Go back and get more, and we do need something to start the fire with. Get a lighter and lighter fluid!"

George said he went back into the store, got three more gallons of kerosene, the lighter, and fluid. He said it took them about ten minutes to drive to the office. There he broke into the building, poured all six gallons of kerosene all over the areas of the office where the IOU could have been, set the fire, and they left.

The detective did a very crucial thing at this point. He said, "I will make you a material witness if you will agree to testify against Wanda. I will see if we can get the lowest charge possible against you if you will agree to this."

George eventually agreed and gave a full statement to the detective. The only problem that would come back and haunt us later is that he did not take a recorded statement, just a written one. I always take a recorded statement, but this was his case, and I did not want to interfere.

The detective went to the prosecutor and eventually convinced a judge to issue an extradition warrant for Wanda in the adjoining state.

We went to Wanda's boss, Dr. Dan, and got a statement from him. He admitted to the affair and the IOU and stated that the file he had it in was destroyed in the fire. He confirmed that the amount she owed him was $20,000.

It is great when you have a subject that gives you a story about what occurred. When you also get creditable evidence to back up his story that is the icing on the cake.

Within days, Wanda was arrested for arson and put in jail. She did not fight the extradition charge and was brought back the state where the crime was committed.

A preliminary hearing occurred with Wanda pleading not guilty to the charges. She was eventually released after her father came and posted her bail of $10,000. Prior to her being released and before she had an attorney, I went to the jail and interviewed her. She denied any of the allegations against her, stated that George was not her boyfriend, that she did not have an affair with Dr. Dan, did not owe him any money, and did not set the fire or have anything to do with setting the fire. I can remember her saying, "If George is all you have to convict me, and you have nothing."

We received several calls from George stating that he was becoming afraid for his own safety and that Wanda's father was a powerful man in the area.

We advised him to stay away from Wanda and the rest of her family and the detective would help him get a restraining order from the judge to protect him.

A trial date was set for the end of the next month, and it did not look good for Wanda. I received a call four days later from the detective I was working with, telling me something very bad had happened. He said that the case against Wanda would probably have to be dropped and that George had been shot and killed.

I was in shock. I asked him what happened, and he said that the story, according to the sheriff in the adjoining state, was that George got drunk, was packing a gun, and went to the house where Wanda lived out in the country at her parents' house. He drove up in the yard and was calling out to Wanda to come out, that he would kill her. Wanda's father went out on the front porch, facing George with a 12-gauge shotgun in his hands. He supposedly told George to leave, George pointed a handgun at the father, and the father shot and killed him right there in the yard.

I asked the detective if he believed the story, and he said, "No way. Something is really wrong here." He said, "Why would George go to the house of Wanda when he called us and said he was afraid what they would do to him for agreeing to testify against her?"

The sheriff in the adjoining state assured our detective that this was clearly a case of justifiable homicide and his case was closed.

The detective I was working with said he had no choice but to go to the prosecutor and get the charges dropped against Wanda, because our star witness was now dead and there went the entire case.

I argued that we had his statement about what had happened and it was backed up by Dr. Dan. The detective stated that a jury in his town would laugh us out of the courtroom with only that evidence.

The charges against Wanda were immediately dropped.

I however, could not let this one go. For one thing, I still had an interest in seeing her convicted, or at least acquire more evidence to go after her civilly. We had paid $150,000 to have the office we insured rebuilt after the fire. I knew Wanda came from a wealthy family, and if I could get enough evidence to subrogate against her, we could get our $150,000 back. Subrogation is when we go to court and file suit against a person to pay us back civilly for any claim we have paid out, showing them to be the wrongdoer.

This is where Joe Momma came in.

Joe Momma had been a police officer in a city nearby for about ten years, and I eventually persuaded him to come work for me. Joe Momma is a big guy and one not to be messed with. We decided to do our own investigation of the shooting.

We went to the home of George and interviewed his father. He was very upset and very willing to speak to us. He kept saying, "They killed my boy. They killed my boy!"

The father said that his son had been in some minor scrapes with the law but he was a good kid and would never hurt anyone. He said that his son had told him about the fire and he would be willing to testify. I told him that would be hearsay evidence and would not be allowed in court.

He said that the story about the shooting of his son was just plain "bull." He said that George had received a call from Wanda's father, asking him to come to the house that night. George's father told his son he was crazy for going, but George was in love with Wanda and wasn't thinking straight when he left. I asked the father if George had a gun in the car when he left. His father said George never carried a gun in the car and he didn't own a gun. The father owned many guns, but all of his were accounted for.

He said this was how he knew that George was murdered, because from the time George left the house and arrived at the house of Wanda's parents, he didn't have time to stop anywhere before the shooting. He said that they set George up and killed him so he couldn't testify.

The father kept begging me, "Please prove that they killed him and he didn't have a gun."

We decided to go to the adjoining state, speak with the sheriff who handled the shooting, and tell the sheriff that according to George's dad, he didn't have a gun when he left the house.

We arrived at the sheriff's office and were asked what we needed by the receptionist. We told the receptionist we needed to speak with the sheriff about the shooting and we had new evidence for him to consider. The sheriff made us wait about twenty minutes before he would speak with us.

He eventually asked us to come into his office, and the first thing he said was, "Why are you proceeding with this investigation? It is an open-and-shut case!" The sheriff said he had known Wanda's father all of his life and they were good friends. He also said that George was nothing but a troublemaker. I knew at that moment we were in big trouble, but I had to tell him what we had uncovered in our investigation. I wish now we would have left at that time.

I told him about the statement we had taken from George's father and the fact that George didn't have a gun. The sheriff said that it was clear that his father was lying because very shortly after the shooting occurred, he received a call from Wanda's father, and the sheriff went to the scene himself to investigate.

He said that when he arrived, George had an old gun in his hand and after the shooting, he examined it himself and it didn't have any serial numbers on it, so it could not be traced.

I asked him what Wanda's father said happened. He said that Wanda's father told him that George came into their yard with the gun in his hand and approached the front porch. When the gun was pointed at Wanda's father, he shot George with a shotgun.

I asked the sheriff if there were photos that were taken of George's body. He got a weird sort of smile on his face and said, "If I show you the photos, will you close your case?"

I told him I didn't know until I saw the photos.

The sheriff brought up on his computer photos of George's body at the scene laying in the yard and then more photos showing George nude in the morgue.

I looked at the photos for a long time, and I knew something wasn't right. Then it hit me.

I asked the sheriff, "If Wanda's father said that George approached him in the yard from the front, pulled a gun, and pointed it at him, why is there powder burns on George's body, which would indicate a close-range shooting? But more than that, George was shot from the side and not the front."

The sheriff got a very weird look on his face, leaned back in his chair, and smiled at both of us.

He then reached over, picked up his phone, and said something into it. The next thing Joe Momma and I knew, the door opened and seven deputies came into the room, surrounding us from the back in sort of a semicircle.

They were all in uniform and armed, and they were not smiling. I looked at Joe Momma, and he had the same thought that I did; I could read it on his face. That thought was, *we are in big trouble*!

The sheriff, without even looking at us, said to one deputy, "Bruce, I want you to tell these here two boys what happened to the last guy that came into my county and started causing trouble."

Bruce said, "Well, Sheriff, someone took him out into the woods, and no one ever saw him again."

Neither one of us had brought a firearm into the sheriff's office with us. We had two in the car, but that was not going to do us a lot of good sitting in chairs in front of the sheriff with his seven henchmen standing behind us.

The sheriff then casually said to us, "Boys, I want you to listen real close to what I am going to tell you. Wanda's father is a close friend of mine. Wanda is a friend of mine. I was there the night of the shooting. I saw what happened, and it is just like Wanda's dad said it was. Now, I want you to think real hard about how you are going to answer my next question, because your life may depend on it. I want you to just say yes or no to this question. Number one, are you going to close your investigation of this case right now? And number two, are you going to get into your car, leave my county immediately, and never, ever come back here again?"

I looked at Joe Momma and saw that he was just about as white as I was. I answered for both of us.

"Sheriff, the answers to your two questions are yes and yes. If you don't mind, we will be leaving now, and you will never hear or see us again."

He said, "Mr. Morgan, you have just made a wise choice."

We got into our car and drove the speed limit to the county line, never looked back, and never spoke to one each other until we got across the state line.

To this day I have not crossed the boundaries of that county, and I do not intend to.

Now, I want you to review all of the facts that I have discussed with this case, and you—not me—make a determination of this one question. Was it justifiable homicide or murder? I am not making any statement about this, ever. I am not even giving my opinion, you can think what you want, but you were not in that chair.

Oh, by the way, Joe Momma agrees with me to this day.

LOETTA

This is my wife's favorite story, and that says a lot, because I have told her many. We still bring it up from time to time with our friends, and even when it is just the two of us, we still think back on this one and bust out laughing. This case involved Loetta, who was the mother of our insured, Marvin.

Let's talk about the case itself, and then I will describe Loetta and her family.

The case was in a small southern town, and it involved a house that caught on fire about midnight on a Friday night. I received the call from our adjuster, and she said the fire department had classified the fire as accidental. I asked her why she called me. She said that she had attended my class on detection of deception and when she sat down with Marvin to take his statement about a fire at his house, she thought he was possibly lying to her. I asked her specifically what he had done. She said that he was hesitant on his answers and he answered a lot of her questions with a question. The biggest reason she wanted me to get involved was that the insured was a real jerk. That was enough for me to start a case on, but she followed it up with this: "The insured is not just a jerk; he is a real jerk."

That really perked me up, because this adjuster doesn't usually get upset with anyone, but she was really upset at Marvin. She actually was afraid of him and did not want to meet with him alone again.

One thing I would like to discuss at this point is that in SIU, we are also occasionally the bodyguard, or protector, of our claims representatives. Most of the time it is with a female adjuster, but there are times I have also gone out to work with a male adjuster just because he was really uncomfortable meeting with an insured or was actually afraid for his own safety.

You have to remember, our adjusters are just that, adjusters. They are not former police officers and for the most part have not been in the military. They are trained to handle claims, and that is it. When they get a claim that involves someone like Marvin, who is a "jerk," they will call us to go with them to the claim or to provide backup when they meet with the insured or claimant.

We have had adjusters threatened, physically harmed, followed, their cars vandalized, their wives threatened, and their houses burned to the ground. Yes, I said burned to the ground. This was a case where the adjuster denied the insured's claim; they found out where our adjuster lived and they fire-bombed his home. It was fortunate that he and his family were not home. I have also stood 24/7 protection with five other SIU brothers, all of us armed, protecting a home of an adjuster when we thought the threat was serious enough to do so. A lot of times, the adjuster just wants you there for backup, especially in an area that is really bad and dangerous.

You must remember one thing: when someone is desperate, they think they can file an insurance claim and get a check. They can take care of the problem and even have some startup money left over. They are pretty upset with us when we do not give them the check immediately. They really get upset when call them and ask for an interview with our adjuster. Then they get more upset when they get called in for an SIU interview. When we have them come in for an examination under oath, they are about ready to become unglued. If we later deny their claim, that is when our job becomes really dangerous.

As I said earlier, I have worked claims before where the police were so concerned that they checked to see if I had a contract out on me. This is usually when a case starts to get really interesting. Sometimes the insured will hire an attorney as soon as I call them for an interview, but most times they wait until they are asked to come in for an examination under oath. This is when you really get their attention.

This is where my great dislike of attorneys starts. I have only met about four or five attorneys in my career that I would sit down and break bread with.

Usually when we asked the insured to come in for examination under oath, they run out and get an attorney to represent them. They meet with their attorney, and he promises the client that he will make the insurance company pay and will even sue them for bad faith and possibly get them a million dollars.

What I am saying is that the majority of insurance companies treat people as they would want to be treated, are very fair, and when they have a claim that deserves to be paid, it is paid. Insurance companies payments vs. denials are about 99 percent paid and 1 percent are denied. After the deposition stage and trial stage of the 1 percent, most of them were compromised in some way. Attorneys usually demand one-third of what they recover for the insured, and this can be a lot of money. In a medical case it can be as high as 50 percent. They will look for any small detail that they think we might have overlooked or missed in our investigation to get us to bend to their will so that they can get a large settlement and get their third.

The bad thing is that almost all of their clients (in my opinion, based on experience, about 90 percent) are submitting fraudulent claims, have stolen from their employer, have burned their house or business to the ground, have had their car stolen and burned, or have staged multiple car or fake fall-down accidents. They even stage fake burglaries at their homes, and the worst thing about it is the attorney knows this and still represents them. They then try to find out anything that we did wrong so he can sue us for bad faith and get a large settlement, all the while knowing what his client has done and making us look like the bad guys.

Even though I dislike most attorneys, I guess our society has to have them in order to keep innocent people from going to jail, but sometimes I wonder how most of them sleep at night.

Let's get back to Marvin, the jerk. I started the investigation by hiring a cause-and-origin investigator. I arranged for the insured to meet with us at his house, and we did our investigation of the fire scene. The insured followed us around like a little puppy dog and kept saying, "Why are you guys doing this? The fire department already said that it was electrical or something." I thought it was really funny while we were there when the insured said to me, "Are you saying that I am a suspect?" I said yes. He said, "I cannot believe that you are accusing me of setting this fire!" I told him that I never said he had set the fire; I just said he was a suspect. I then told him that the only person that I knew who didn't set his fire was me, because I knew I didn't do it.

He hesitated for a moment, and then I went for it. I said, "Did you set this fire?"

He said, "You're asking me if I set this fire?"

That was a huge mistake on his part.

Avinoam Sapir teaches in his SCAN class that when someone answers a question with a question, it is total, 100 percent deception. In this case, Marvin answered my question with a question. Oops, guilty!

I told him that we had to determine what caused the fire, because if it was something someone did that started the fire; we may have recourse against them for subrogation. I also told him if someone set the fire, then we would want to find out who did. Immediately he again became defensive and said, "Are you saying that I set this fire?"

At that point it was like July 4th going off in my head about the insured's question. I had not accused him of anything, and he was already this defensive? Something was really wrong here. He also became very agitated and uncooperative at that point. You are asking yourself, what is wrong with that? He just had a fire at his house. I have found that if an insured is innocent, they will want you to find the cause of the fire, and if someone set the fire, they want the person discovered and punished. This was not the case with Marvin. Instead of the normal insured being cooperative and wanting to do anything to help, Marvin was just, a total uncooperative "jerk."

During my career as a cop and then as an insurance investigator, I have always tried to live by this rule: If a person is nice to me and cooperative, I will bend over backward for them to prove they didn't do anything wrong, even if the evidence was against them. But if you are a jerk, then God have mercy on you, because I will come after you with a vengeance and not leave a stone turned over during the investigation, because this is not normal and something is really wrong.

My cause-and-origin expert told me right away that we had an arson fire, and I agreed with him. It had been made to look like an electrical fire, but there were three points of origin, and at one point of origin, the fire burned around a corner. I cannot believe that the fire investigator for the city did not see this. Fires do not burn around corners unless gasoline has been poured in that fashion to make the fire turn while it is burning the gas. It cannot do that on its own. It will just burn up and out in a room, and that is the natural progression.

We then called in an arson dog from the state, and he arrived within a few hours. The dog got three hits for accelerants in the house. My cause-and-origin expert took samples and said he would send them to the lab for analysis.

I told the insured that the fire was arson and I would be contacting him in the next few days for a recorded statement. I asked him if he had any enemies, and he immediately said that if anyone burned it down, it had to be Steve. I asked him who Steve was, and he said that his little sister had married this pervert who was also married in California to another woman. He said that he and Steve had words more than once about him marrying his sister, because Steve was thirty-two and his sister was thirteen. His little sister had actually obtained permission from his mother, Loetta, for the marriage to occur. They already had one child, and another one was on the way. I know this is hard to believe, but in this area of the country, this is not that unusual. I asked him where Steve lived, and he said that Steve lived with Marvin's mother in a trailer in the woods outside of town. I asked him the name of his mother, and he said Loetta.

I knew the sheriff really well in this county, and I went there next to try to find out anything I could about this family.

The sheriff said, "Oh my God, where do I start?"

He said that Marvin was, in most people's eyes, looked up to as an outstanding member of the community, but he thought otherwise. He said Marvin was the head of the soccer program for the kids in the city, and he was very involved. The sheriff then told me that he thought that Marvin had killed his own father. For clarification, he thought Marvin killed his own father, not the sheriff's father. This occurred after Marvin discovered that his father was very ill and didn't have long to live. The sheriff told me that he had been told that the father of Marvin was mad at him about some of the things he had been doing and saying about the family. He had also heard that prior to this; Marvin was the person who would receive the largest part of the inheritance on the death of his father. He had also been told that the father was going to change his will, leaving Marvin with nothing, and Marvin was aware of this.

The sheriff said that before the will was changed, Marvin's father had committed suicide. I asked what the specifics were, and he said the city handled this case, investigated it, and closed the case as a suicide. He said just based on what he had heard, if he had had the case, the outcome would have been totally different because he didn't think it was a suicide.

I asked him why he thought that. He said, "All I am going to tell you is this. His father supposedly was standing at the top of his basement stairs the day before he was going to change his will, took a twelve-gauge shotgun, held it in his hands, pointed the barrel at his mouth, and pulled the trigger. He was found at the bottom of the basement stairs with the shotgun lying on top of him and his head blown off."

He said that at the time, Marvin's father had been divorced from Loetta, Marvin's mother, for about five years, and the will gave Marvin everything. The changed will was never found, and Marvin received all of the money after his father's death.

He said there wasn't a lot, maybe $30,000, but Marvin got it all.

He said, "You need to be careful nosing around this town, because Marvin has ears everywhere, and he has contacts and relatives all over the city, including the police department." I wish I had listened to this a lot closer at the time, and you will find out later in this chapter why.

He then told me about Marvin's family, and this is a story all in itself.

He said Marvin had been married to a Linda, but she divorced him about a year before. Marvin had not remarried. He said, "Be careful when you visit Loetta. She is a rough one, stands about six feet two, has no teeth, and could whip most of the men in the town." He also said that she raised pit bulls and fighting cocks.

He said that where she lived was in the middle of nowhere in a trailer in the middle of the woods.

He said that there were about three families living with Loetta. He said that Loetta was about fifty and she was living with a young guy, about twenty. Then there was Steve, who was a crook who had married Loretta's thirteen-year-old daughter, and the sheriff said he thought Steve might be about thirty. Then the sheriff said there were two other sisters, one of which was married, and she was maybe fifteen and also pregnant, and they were all living together in this small trailer.

He said that he knew that Steve had been locked up for bigamy, but he wasn't sure about all of the specifics about that.

I then decided to touch base with the fire department. I met with their arson investigator, whom I didn't like from the start. He said that he didn't see any problem with the fire and it was accidental. I told him what we had discovered, that the fire was arson, and he said, "Well, when you get done with your investigation, I will get you a letter, then you can give me a copy of the investigation and I will take a look at it."

In the state that I was working this fire, there is a state law that if the fire department asks you for a copy of your file, you have no choice but to comply. I knew he would be of no help to me.

I also had checked with the state arson investigator, and he said that he could not get involved unless the city asked him to come in and investigate.

I called back the arson investigator for the city, and he said he didn't see any need to call in the State Fire Marshal and he could handle the investigation. He stated that he really wanted to get whoever did this if it was arson.

I then decided to start checking on Marvin a little more. I did sort of a town canvas, and everyone I spoke with said that he was a great guy, did everything for the kids in the town in the soccer program, and was well respected. I started getting concerned at that point. The insured may have set this fire, and if I went for a denial of the claim and the insured filed suit, the jury pool would be from people who thought he walked on water. I knew I had a huge problem going into this one.

I then decided to go and see if Marvin's ex-wife would speak to me. I went to her house, and she came to the door very slowly. She was a young woman about thirty but walked like she was eighty and acted that way also. She asked me in, and I asked her if I could take a statement from her regarding her ex-husband

and anything that she knew about the fire. She agreed and proceeded to tell me that Marvin was a total jerk. I was starting to get a mixed picture of dear old' Marvin at this point.

She stated that they had been married for several years and everything was good until she developed acute crippling rheumatoid arthritis. She said that she got to the point that even sex hurt her and she had to decline Marvin's advances. He became infuriated many times and would beat her. She said that three times she was injured so badly that she had to go to the hospital for treatment, and the last time when he actually picked her up, threw her into a wall, and broke several bones, she left and eventually divorced him.

I started seeing a possibility of swaying a jury with this one, but I would have to see how the case played out. I had just discovered the true side of Marvin.

I received a call from the arson investigator, and he said that he interviewed a witness who said on the night of the fire he saw a red pickup truck leaving the scene, and the description of the white male inside could have been Steve, the brother-in-law of Marvin. He said that Steve did have a red truck.

I agreed to meet with this witness and the arson investigator. It was obvious to me that the witness knew the arson investigator and that they had spoken at length about the situation. Using the interviewing techniques that I teach every day, I soon recognized that the witness was lying through his teeth, and the worst part about it was that the arson investigator was assisting him in the lie.

I took his statement, made it a part of my file, and thanked him for the information.

He said he was driving by Marvin's house about ten o'clock at night. The fire started at about ten fifteen, according to my own arson cause-and-origin person, and also by a trick that I have used for many years. I knew what time (within twenty to thirty minutes) that the fire started. I do this by carrying with me a simple pocket knife. I go to the heaviest amount of charring, or "alligatoring."

Alligatoring is what you see happen to wood when you are sitting around a campfire. The wood starts to change on its surface, and it looks like the back of an alligator. The longer the wood burns, the easier it is to stick a knife into it. I then stick the knife into the wood, and for every inch that the knife goes into the charring easily, you can pretty well take it to the bank that is one hour of actual burn time before the fire department puts the fire out. Using this technique, I was able to determine that the fire started between ten and ten thirty.

The witness stated that he was just driving by the house at about ten o'clock. He said he thought it was unusual that he saw a man running from the house and getting into a red pickup truck.

The arson investigator had now changed his mind about the fire being electrical and stated that he thought he knew who was driving the red truck, and his name was Steve Smith. He said he knew Steve and he was a worthless individual. He said that he would now gear his investigation toward Steve.

I grew very concerned at this point that I had some type of conspiracy going on, because I knew the arson investigator for the city and the witness were feeding me a line of crap. I couldn't figure out why the investigator was protecting our insured, because I had suspicions at this point that our insured may have set the fire.

I decided it was time to meet Loetta and Steve.

This proved to be an enlightening experience that I will never forget.

I went to the sheriff's department and asked for directions to Loetta's home.

He told me to be very careful when I got there and not to get out of the car until Loetta came out and said that it was okay. I asked him why; he just laughed and said, "You will see."

I drove to the area where the sheriff directed me, and it was in the middle of nowhere.

I left the main road and traveled for about three-quarters of a mile on a dirt road, eventually going up to the top of a small hilly area. I finally broke out into a clearing, and what I saw, I did not expect. There was a broken-down trailer in the middle of a clearing, and there were about twelve pit bull dogs that had already surrounded my car and were snapping at the tires. Some of them were very large, and some were small. I didn't see anyone around, so I started beeping my horn. While I was doing this, hoping that the dogs didn't bite through my tires, I looked behind the trailer and saw several small houses, like doghouses, but beside each house was a rooster, which later I would discover were fighting cocks.

I know many of you that are reading this are shocked at this, but in this part of the country it is illegal, but it is happening every day, and it is like going to a casino for those in the northern states. The sheriffs of these counties usually handle the admission fee and charge parking.

It was obvious to me that Loetta was heavily involved in both aspects of the local sport of pit bull and cock fighting. The one really sick thing I learned was that they would attach razor-like implements to the feet of the roosters before the fight, and when they were paired off in the ring, they would attack each other and slice at each other with the razors on their feet, and the fight was only over when one was dead. I heard that the breeding for this type of bird was expensive and one bird could cost several thousand dollars for the owner to purchase.

Eventually Loetta came out of her house. She was a very large woman with hair tied back behind her head. She had no teeth, and at first glance I thought to myself, *you are in big trouble* and, *I would not want to meet this woman in a dark alley*. She came toward my car from the trailer and started yelling at the dogs and kicking at them. Some would roll several times from the kick, and others would stay just enough out of reach so the kick missed them. It was obvious to me that Loetta was in total control and the dogs were in mortal fear of her. The words coming out of her mouth would have made many sailors flinch.

She eventually got close to my car and asked, "What do you want? Are you the law?"

I was in a red Ford Crown Victoria, which the state police used in this state as their undercover cars.

I immediately rolled down my window and told her that I was an insurance investigator and I needed to talk to her about Marvin's fire that I was investigating. She immediately changed from the Wicked Witch of the West into a smiling, almost friendly person.

She said, "We have been waiting for you. We have a lot to talk about!"

She told me it was okay to get out of the car, and she played interference for me all the way to the trailer, kicking any growling dog that would come close to me and sending them rolling. Eventually, the dogs got the message and stayed away from the deadly boots she was wearing.

She asked me to come into the trailer, and I was very reluctant at this point. I was very surprised when inside. The trailer was very well used but organized and clean. No dogs were in the house, thank goodness. There were, however, about eight people in the trailer, and to this day I still don't know where they all slept. In the outside area they had built sort of an enclosed patio, which was screened in, and this was where the picnic table was that we sat at. I eventually learned that this was really the kitchen area where they all ate, and the table would seat about twelve.

Loetta introduced herself to me and said that Marvin was her son, but he was a no-good, rotten SOB. She said that her husband had supposedly committed suicide, but even though they had been divorced for years, she knew that this was not true. She said she had always suspected Marvin of killing her ex-husband.

She said she had three daughters who all lived with her, and there were several children of all ages in the trailer. The oldest mother I saw appeared to be about fifteen.

There must have been four or five children running around, none older than three.

Loetta said that there was no doubt that Marvin set the fire and she would testify to this at any trial. She said that Marvin needed the money and he was not the great, civic, prided citizen that everyone thought he was.

She said that he had even mentioned to her that he would burn the house if he needed more money.

She asked if I had spoken with his ex-wife, and I told her I had.

Loetta said that she was now married to a nineteen-year-old, and she introduced me to him. Loetta was about fifty-six or fifty-seven years old but looked about sixty-five.

Loetta then introduced me to her son-in-law, Steve. I thought, *Wow, this is like killing two birds with one stone.* Steve turned out to be a thirty-seven-year-old who was married to Loretta's thirteen-year-old daughter. They had one child, about a year old, and the thirteen-year-old daughter bride was pregnant again.

I asked if I could speak with Steve at the picnic table for a while. Steve turned out to be a pretty nice guy, although during the interview I asked him if he had ever been arrested, and he said yes, for bigamy. He said, "I served my time in jail because the girl I was supposedly married to in California was not true because the marriage was never legal."

He said that Marvin had told the police about him, they had checked with the authorities, and he had been arrested. He said he spent thirty days in jail. He said that eventually everything got cleared up. I asked him about the so-called California marriage, and he said that the paperwork wasn't filed right and they had not been married by a real preacher, even though he left the girl pregnant in California—but he did feel bad about that.

I then asked Steve if he or anyone else in the trailer family had set the fire. He immediately said no, and I did not see any deception in him at all. Steve was just a good old' boy who lived under entirely different rules and morals than I was used to—but again, I am not one to judge.

I explained to Steve that a witness had given me a statement saying that he saw Steve leave the house that burned belonging to Marvin just before the fire started.

Steve then gave me the biggest break I had in this case thus far. I could not have asked for anything any better unless it were served on a platter.

Steve said, "Let me guess, the fire investigator from the city came to you with this witness, right?"

I told him that was true but I could not reveal who it was. He then told me the name of my witness. I asked him how he knew that. He said that he was surprised that no one had told me this before, but the fire investigator was Marvin's cousin and they were lifelong friends. He said the witness was another cousin who was a fishing buddy of Marvin's.

I again asked Steve if he had set the fire. He said, "Well, I had thought about it, but then I knew that Marvin had insurance money, so if I set the fire, I would just be doing him a favor."

This case was several years ago, but based on what Steve told me that day, I have asked this question on every arson fire I had since, and I think you will realize why after I tell you the question.

The question is (asked to the insured that owns the house that burned): "Who, other than yourself, would profit in any way by your house burning?"

The usual answer is, "Well, no one that I can think of." Then they sit there, and they realize what they have said. If there was no one else that would profit from it, who else would have burned their house? It is at this point that they get this really weird look on their face, and if they had been combative up to that point, they are not any longer and for some reason become very humble.

I then asked Steve the question that he would repeat his answer six months later in a courtroom. "Where were you on the night of the fire?"

He said, "Jack, I was in jail."

I said, "What?"

He again said, "On the night of the fire, I was in jail in an adjoining county on the bigamy charge."

I asked him if he would get any paperwork on this for me, and he said he would check with the sheriff and get his release papers.

I asked him not to tell that to anyone if he was asked, and he said it would be our little secret.

I also took a statement from Loetta, and she confirmed all that Steve had told me about the cousins, the fire investigator, etc.

I was finally starting to realize one thing: I had been set up from the beginning, and all of the cousins were covering for Marvin.

The fire arson investigator had covered up evidence, the fact that the fire was arson, and he refused to call in the State Fire Marshal, brought me fake witnesses, even stating that they had seen Steve in his red truck, and that he left the house, running, at the time of the fire How could Steve be in two places at the same time?

I then realized that everyone except Loetta, Steve, and the ex-wife of Marvin had been leading me on a wild goose chase. Why would everyone be doing this?

The only reason was that Marvin had set the fire.

I then started to get really serious about this fire investigation. I called for a backup from our home office to assist me in the investigation. I called in Al, or "Hackman."

When Al arrived, I brought him up to date on the investigation, and we worked a very long day checking witnesses and tracking down lead after lead.

I call this "shaking the bushes." The reason I do this is so that everyone I speak with will report back to Marvin as to what I did and what I asked, because it was such a small town, and evidently I was right.

We checked into a hotel on the outskirts of town. It was a pretty nice hotel, and I was starting to get a little gun shy at this point. I instructed the hotel manager that no matter who called and asked if we were there, he was not supposed to tell anyone that we were staying there.

About nine o'clock in the evening, Al and I were in my room going over the day's investigation and comparing notes. I got a call on the hotel room phone. I picked it up, and it was Steve. He said, "Jack, listen to me, you need to get out of town right away and leave your hotel. They know where you are, and tonight they are going to fire bomb your rooms." And he hung up.

We immediately packed up our bags and went to the front desk. I asked the front desk clerk why he had given our number to Steve. He said that Steve said it was an emergency. I asked him if anyone else had called, and he said, "Yes, the fire investigator called and wanted to know if you were here."

So much for privacy and trusting a hotel clerk.

I told him that we would not pay for the rooms, and we left. We drove about thirty miles out of town, checked into another hotel, and didn't get much sleep that night.

We finished the investigation, and after the evidence was reviewed by the home office, we decided to hire an attorney to conduct an examination under oath of Marvin. An examination under oath is where our attorney, Marvin's attorney and I meet with a court reporter present. Marvin showed up with his attorney and was asked questions, and his answers were recorded by the court reporter.

One very interesting thing happened at the EUO with Marvin. He thought he was several things, one was a lady killer—I mean that in a Casanova sort of way—and the second thing was he thought he was a really bad dude.

In one break when our attorneys left the room and the court reporter was gone, Marvin and I were left alone in the room. He leaned over the table and said, "The first day I met you, I should have kicked your butt and thrown you into the street."

Being the diplomatic person I am, I just looked at him and said, "Marvin, the only thing that is in between us right now is this table. Don't let it stop you. Bring it on." Marvin backed down and left the room.

The biggest thing we got from the EUO was that Marvin did not have an alibi. He said that he was working all night and whenever they left work they had to clock in and clock out and there was no way that he could have set the fire if he was at work. I had already checked with the insured's foreman, and he had told me he was very lax about this rule. If someone wanted to leave for about twenty minutes, he never made them clock out, and he even remembered that Marvin had left that night for about twenty minutes and had not clocked out. When we asked Marvin about this in the EUO, he stated that he had not left work. This is very crucial to this investigation and the ultimate decision that we made to deny this claim.

Marvin worked about five minutes from his home. He could have easily left work and set his house on fire then returned to work thinking he had an airtight alibi, but he didn't plan on me interviewing his boss.

The EUO ended in some good information, but not as much as I usually like to take a case to trial. When I take a case to trial, I like for it to be airtight. This case had a lot going for it, but it was not there yet in my opinion.

You have to remember, we were in a southern town that probably hates insurance companies, and this guy was the little league soccer hero.

We left the EUO with some good stuff, and Marvin had told me he wanted to kick my butt, but he had backed down.

Later I told my attorney what occurred, and he gave me a high-five.

My attorney still tells this next story about what happened whenever I see him, no matter who we are around. My attorney was doing some follow-up investigation with me one day in the city, and I got a call from a guy I didn't know. It turned out to be Marvin's brother. He said he had information for me and wanted to meet.

I called Steve and asked him about the brother. Steve said, "Watch your rear!" He said that Marvin's brother was a bad dude and had been arrested many times for beatings, shootings, etc. and always carried a gun.

I knew that the brother would probably not give me a recorded statement, so I asked my attorney, Ed, "Do you want to wear the wire or carry the gun?"

Ed did not hesitate. He said, "I will wear the wire."

We drove to the brother's house, and I was very cautious about a setup. It was obvious that the brother did have a gun on, but it was also obvious that we were not in any danger only after about two minutes with him. He did not like Marvin at all, and he was trying to help us bust Marvin.

Marvin's brother told us that there was no doubt in his mind that his brother had set this fire, and he also said that he knew that his brother had killed his father and wanted him to at least not get paid for the fire claim. He said to be careful with the city arson investigator, because he was working with Marvin. I told him I realized this.

My attorney has never let me forget the situation I put him into that day, but he was convinced that we could win this case at trial, and at this point I had a 100 percent conviction or win rate with him. We had never lost a case, which was pretty unbelievable for an insurance company.

We had a phone conference with the home office supervisor, and we debated whether to deny the claim or to pay it. If we denied the claim, which was about $200,000, and we lost, we would probably have to pay the $200,000. There was also the issue of bad faith. If we lost the case, it would mean we would have to pay additional monies for the bad faith if it was shown at the trial. The home office supervisor asked me what I thought our chances were, because I am not allowed to make the final decision on any claim as no payment, denial, or compromise. I told him based on the evidence I had and the area that we were working in, I gave it about a sixty-forty chance of winning.

He asked me if my investigation was completed, and I said that it was. I could not think of any other witnesses to interview. He said, "Do you think Marvin set the fire?"

I said, "There is no doubt in my mind, and if it makes any difference, I think he killed his own father to get the inheritance money."

We had a conference call with our attorney, and he said he felt good about going to trial. He made the final decision, and the denial letter was sent to Marvin's attorney, stating that he had misrepresented his claim, that we thought he had set the fire, and that we were denying his entire claim for contents and the house.

In about two weeks we received a letter from his attorney that was very threatening, and he said if we did not pay the claim immediately, he would file suit for the claim and bad faith.

We stood our ground, and the attorney stuck to his word and filed suit against us for the $200,000, attorney fees, and punitive damages.

The trial was set to occur in three months.

Usually when a suit is filed, the insured's attorney asks for a deposition of many people. Always it includes me, as the investigator, and usually the home office supervisor who denied the claim.

I attended my deposition, and in my entire career this has only happened twice. My entire file that I had given the fire investigator for the city was in the hands of the Marvin's attorney.

This was unforgivable. The file was given to the authorities by law at their request, and it was supposed to assist them in their investigation of the bad guy. In this case, the cousin of the insured gave the insured's attorney my entire file, which listed everything I had done, everyone I had spoken with, and literally my entire investigation.

The insured's attorney had my entire file with him at my deposition. He knew everything about my investigation except for one thing, which proved to be his downfall.

I did not put into any report that Steve was actually in jail at the time of the fire.

Their entire case was based on two main things. One, they said that Steve had set the fire, and two; they thought that no jury in the hometown of the soccer president would find him guilty.

I know you are wondering why I did not seek charges against the insured for arson with the information I had.

Well, I did try but was turned down by the prosecutor, who was also a relative.

The only thing that we could do was deny the claim and hope for a verdict in our favor so the insured would not get any money.

When I realized that the arson investigator had given up my file to the other side, I was totally disgusted with him and told him so. He just shrugged his shoulders and walked away from me.

The time came for the trial, and my case mainly depended on three witnesses: Loetta, the mother of the insured; Steve, the bigamist; and the ex-wife of the insured, whom he had beat up continuously when they were married.

The problem I had was that we ended up with a jury of eight black women and four white men. We had to have a majority verdict to win—not a total one, but a majority.

The eight black women bothered me because their sons or grandsons had probably been on Marvin's soccer team at one time or another.

I also had this going against me: the arson investigator testified that in his opinion, the fire was accidental and that he had told me this.

I had Loetta ready to show up for court and Steve ready at home. The ex-wife was in the courtroom for the two days, hidden in a room away from anyone so no one would know that she was there.

The only time I could use her testimony was if at the end of the trial, the insured put on several character witnesses to show what a good guy he was.

I was called to testify, and I thought I was pretty cool and collected. I had learned one thing from watching tapes of Saddam Hussein. When he was being interviewed by Dan Rather prior to the invasion, Saddam didn't have any paper in front of him. He had a pen. He would constantly click and un-click this pen when he was questioned about something that bothered him or was stressful. I realized that it was a prop and he was using the pen to relieve stress.

When you testify in a courtroom, it is the most stressful thing you can ever do. When you walk into the courtroom, the judge, bailiff, attorneys, jurors, spectators, court recorder, and the insured are all watching you. Are you presentable, trustworthy, too cocky, too overdressed, or do you just stand too straight or not stand straight at all?

Everyone is sizing you up from the time you walk in until you are sworn in and begin your testimony.

The stress is unbelievable. I walked into the courtroom to testify with my silent clicking pen in my hand. I discussed this technique in an earlier chapter, "Testifying In The Courtroom."

I thought I did a very good job of testifying, but I could feel bad vibes from the jury. I started thinking for the first time, *It doesn't matter to anyone if he set the fire or not. He is going to win.*

I confirmed this with the court bailiff. They are the best ones to go to if you want to know if you are winning or not. They do this every day. They can read juries and can tell you who is going to win the trial at the time you ask them based on the testimony at that point. I would say that a court bailiff can tell you who is going to win a case before the jury comes back 99 percent of the time.

During a break I went to the bailiff and asked, "Well, what do you think?"

He said, "You have lost this one." I was devastated. How could this guy get away with this? The bailiff was telling me we had lost, and I hadn't had one witness on the stand yet.

It was finally time for Loetta to testify. I called and told her to be in the courtroom at one o'clock.

About twelve thirty, Loetta showed up, but she was not alone.

She was with another woman, and they were hugging and kissing and all over each other in the courtroom.

I went up to her with our attorney and said, "Loetta, what is going on?"

She said as honestly as she knew how, "Jack, all my life I have been living a lie. I have thrown the young pup I was living with out of the house, and I finally realize that I am a lesbian," and she continued to hug, kiss on the lips, and caress her newfound lover.

I thought, *oh my God, the bailiff is telling me I am losing this case, now Loetta has changed sexual preferences midstream, and with a jury of eight black women, this is not going to be good.*

I discussed the situation with my attorney, and he said he thought it best to excuse Loetta from testifying in the courtroom.

The next witness was Steve. I planned on using Steve as a rebuttal once the other side told that their theory was that Steve had burned the home and they could prove it.

They brought in many witnesses that stated that Marvin was a good guy, etc.

They said that Steve had no alibi, and they said we did not interview him, and that would be bad faith against us if the jury found in their favor. I looked at the eight black women on the jury, and now instead of them smiling at me, they were frowning.

I called Steve and told him to come into the courtroom, that we needed him in rebuttal.

He said his car had broken down and he had no way to get there.

I told him I would be there to pick him up. We asked for a recess, and I picked Steve up and delivered him to the courtroom.

You have to know the elation on my face when Steve testified that at the time of the fire he was in jail in a neighboring county for bigamy. They didn't believe him, but I had asked Steve to bring in the release and actual lockup time for the bigamy charge.

The record showed that Steve was in jail during the time period that the fire was set.

The attorney for Marvin about dropped his jaw when we showed him records on the night of the fire that Steve was actually in jail.

I have not seen the prosecutor many times since that day, and he probably doesn't want to see me because of different implications that it could reveal.

Okay, so I have in my favor the fact that the insured possibly could have left this workplace, but not totally. I have to get the jury to buy this evidence first, and it didn't look good.

So what evidence did I really have?

I had Loetta, but I could not put her on the stand. I could not get her away from her newly found lover long enough.

I had Steve and the ex-wife. All Steve's testimony did was prove that he didn't set the fire. He had been in jail.

I looked at the bailiff, and he was shaking his had no; this meant I was losing the case.

The only hope I had was that the insured's attorney would be stupid enough to parade character witnesses in front of the jury to show what a good guy he really was.

When he brought his first witness, I just smiled, leaned over to my attorney, and told him we had just won this case.

He didn't agree and was very worried at this point.

Once all of the witnesses had testified how great a guy the insured was, it was then our turn for rebuttal.

I had them go get Marvin's ex-wife.

She came hobbling into the courtroom, using a cane, and was bent over. She testified that she had crippling rheumatoid arthritis and that her ex-husband, the great guy that ten character witnesses had said was next to a saint, had beaten her repeatedly in her condition when they were married. She had hospital records with her that we got admitted into evidence where he had beaten her, and an ambulance had to be called three times to take her to the hospital after the beatings.

After she was finished testifying, I looked at the eight women of the jury. Instead of them staring at me and knowing I had lost the case, they were now staring at the insured with great distaste, and I knew we had won.

The jury deliberated after the testimonies for about an hour.

They came back, and the judge asked them if they had a verdict. They did, and it was unanimous. The insured was awarded nothing. They found in favor of my insurance company.

Now I was elated and I knew justice was done that day.

But was it really?

I knew that day that any trial by jury was not based on what the testimony was or what the facts of the case were.

The jury decided the outcome based on what they thought of the witnesses, the insured, etc., based on personalities and what they believed. It had nothing to do with evidence, and this was really a shame, but in this case…

I am so glad they did.

Loetta left with her lover, Steve went back to his thirteen-year-old wife, and the ex-wife went home with a smile on her face that justice had finally been served.

When we came out of the courthouse, my brand-new company car, a Crown Victoria, had a key scratch on both sides of the car from bumper to bumper. The repair bill was $1,000.

My attorney and I left town quickly, drove to the first steakhouse we could find, sixty miles away, had a couple of drinks, and savored the victory.

BUSINESS CARDS

In my line of work, I have developed a habit of passing out my business cards everywhere I go and to every person I come in contact with. The next two short stories are about business cards and how they saved my company a total of about $700,000 for the cost of printing two business cards.

The first claim is one of the dearest to my heart. Out of all the claims I have ever worked or will work, none compare to this one because I was able, through my investigation, to do what the FBI could not do, and at the same time I got a thirteen-year-old girl who was being abused out of that situation and put into a foster home.

At the same time, I saved the company hundreds of thousands of dollars and put several people in jail for a very long time.

I would love to tell you where this occurred and what the names of the people were, but I do not want to embarrass this young girl or hurt her life in any way.

Let's say this claim occurred in a southern town, and let's call the insured's the Johnsons.

I first got involved in the claim when our adjuster called me on an arson fire. This one was a little different from others, because the fire department and sheriff's department also confirmed that this was an arson fire.

It involved a brass shop we had only insured for about a year. The first hint of fraud was when I checked the policy before I even went to the scene. The insured had increased the coverage on the building and the contents by 50 percent just weeks before the fire.

The second red flag I got was when I called the sheriff's department and they told me that one of the insured's, the husband (Mr. Johnson), was in jail for burglary, had been charged, and could not raise his bail.

I drove to the scene of the fire, but before I got there, I received a call from the FBI. They told me that they had been investigating this family for two years. They were suspected of staging insurance fraud accidents over the last two to three years and taking insurance companies for over two and a half million dollars.

I was told that they could not get charges filed against the "family" because they were totally obligated to and protected each other. There were about ten people involved, all relatives and all drug users.

They also told me that the doctor the Johnsons went to for their injuries was reportedly involved, and so was their attorney, who filed all the lawsuits against insurance companies.

They said that they knew I was investigating a fire, but they wanted me to be aware of their investigation.

If the opportunity arose, they wanted me to ask the Johnsons some questions that they could not ask them, because they had an attorney who would not let them answer any of their questions, and they were at a standstill in their investigation. They said anything I could do to help them would be appreciated.

The only problem with their request was that I could not help them. They did not understand that if I did ask the insured their questions in an interview, it could come back and haunt all of us later.

First, any questions that I would have asked for the police without me advising the insured of their Miranda rights would be bad news for everyone. I could be considered an agent of the police department, and if I did not advise them of their rights, any statement they gave to me would not be admissible in court.

I could also be in bad faith with our insured, and that could cost my company millions of dollars.

There were many indicators from the start of this claim that appeared that the Johnsons were being led by an attorney to set us up for bad faith, and anything we did wrong would have come back to haunt us.

I handled this investigation strictly by the book. I have always wondered why attorneys do not try this tactic more. If you intentionally lead the insurance company down a path, hoping they will screw up, it could be very profitable for the insured and their attorney.

An example of this is when I first meet with an insured and they say, "Do I need an attorney?" or, "Do I need to speak with an attorney before I answer our questions?"

If I say, "No, you don't need one," and tell them legal advice regarding speaking to an attorney or not, then I could be charged with practicing law without a license. This would also put my company in bad faith, and the insured could probably file suit against my company and me personally.

The correct answer when someone asks me that question is, "Have you retained an attorney?" If they say no, then I tell them that they do have a right to have an attorney and to speak with an attorney before they answer my questions. If they wish to have an attorney present, I stop the interview and tell them to have their attorney call me and we will reset the appointment.

I do, however, tell them that their policy is a contract and even if they have an attorney, they do have to speak with me and cooperate with my investigation. If they don't do both, then their claim can be denied based on the mutually agreed contract when they took out the policy.

I have had many claims where an insured, if they answer my questions, could go to jail based on their answers if they are involved in some type of criminal activity.

The reason for this is that if I am requested to do so by the police or other authorities, I have to give them a complete copy of my file. If the insured's transcribed statement is in the file, then the police have access to it and the insured can be charged with the crime.

I called Mrs. Johnson and set up a time to meet with her at the fire scene. She refused to meet with me at her home, and that was okay. I cannot force the place of the interview. I can only force them to answer my questions.

This can be written or taped, but they do have to answer questions.

I went to the fire scene and did my walk-through inspection. I found three points of origin for the fire, and this was a no-brainer. It was arson.

I then started looking around at what the inventory in the store should have been, and it appeared to be very much depleted.

I asked to see her books on sales over the last six months, and there was no way she could have stayed in business much longer.

I asked her many questions about the fire—where she was at when the fire occurred, their financial situation, etc.

With her at the time of the statement was her thirteen-year-old daughter.

I have met and dealt with many abused children in my career, especially when I was a highway patrolman, and she fit the category.

She did not speak unless spoken to, never looked at her mother, and cowered when her mother was around. She would not look at me, but I could feel as though she wanted to shout out something to me that was burning inside her heart.

Mrs. Johnson confirmed that her husband was in jail but the charges were all made up against him. She said that her and her daughter had been at the brass shop until about seven o'clock, when they closed down the shop and went home. They were there by themselves until they got the call that a fire had broken out.

I also knew something was really wrong because every time the mother would make a statement, she would look to her daughter and say, "Isn't that right, honey?"

The little girl would not say yes or no; she would just say, "Uh-huh." I have always found that when I ask a question and someone answers with a yes or no, I believe this a lot more than *Uh-huh* or *Uh-uh*. The second thing that she did was a dead give-away. She was saying "uh-huh" (yes) but shaking her head no at the same time. This is total deception.

The fire started about nine o'clock in the evening. You can tell this by the amount of char that is in wood, the time the fire was called in, witnesses, etc. The best evidence of the time the fire was set was because there was a business next door, and he had a few customers left in the store and was getting ready to close about five minutes before nine. He said smoke started coming into his shop, and that was when he called the fire department. The thing that really made me mad about this fire was that the insured set the fire and had total disregard for any safety of anyone. There were occupants on either side of her business, and she set the fire when the buildings were still occupied. Luckily, no one was hurt seriously. If the fire had not been extinguished right away, an entire city block could have also burned.

I asked Mrs. Johnson her name, and she said it was Penny. I then asked her about prior claims, and she denied ever having any. This in itself proved to be a huge misrepresentation, because they had experienced one small fire before, and she had been involved in about thirty other auto claims.

I discovered this when I ran a background check on her and her husband, Fred Johnson. Some of the claims had been denied by companies, others had been paid, others had been denied and gone to trial, and the Johnsons had won almost all of the cases at trial.

I gave Penny several forms to sign, and I handed her my business card.

She said she would have her attorney look them over.

I asked her if she was represented by an attorney on this fire, and she said no; he was just giving her advice, and she had not hired him yet.

Most people who say "yet" are trying to intimidate you. This means, if you pay my claim, no attorney; if you give me any trouble, then I will sic my attorney on you.

In the last part of the statement, I asked the insured (as I do in most of my claims) if she had set the fire. It went like this:

"All the questions you have answered—are all of your answers true?

She said, "Yes."

I then asked her, "Why should I believe what you just told me?"

She laughed and said, "Why shouldn't you?"

This was a double whammy. She committed deception twice; she answered a question with question, and she laughed when there was no reason to laugh. I use this on almost every claim I work. I call it my verbal polygraph test. It is not admissible in court, and I cannot use it in any other way except to narrow my investigation. I usually can tell when and where the person is lying to me based on the five techniques that I use every day in detection of deception.

The correct answer to the question, "Why should I believe what you just told me?" is, "Because it is the truth!"

I left many of my business cards around the fire scene that day in the hopes that someone would pick them up and give me a call if they had any information. I didn't know at the time how important this was to the case and ultimately, the one thing that would break this case wide open.

After I left the insured's business, I received a very important call from the sheriff's department. They wanted me to stop by and get a copy of a letter they had intercepted by randomly reading prisoners' mail. I drove to the sheriff's department, and they gave me a letter that was from Fred to Penny.

It was, to say the least, very enlightening.

The letter was bizarre. It started out with Fred telling Penny how much he loved and missed her, and then it went into a rage over her messing up the claim. He said that she should have done a better job and known they had to go through all this insurance stuff. He then told her that in addition to all of the brass items she had sold at the flea market, she needed to start working the truck stops again to get more money so she could bail him out. I will leave that to your imagination.

The odd part of the letter was that he never mentioned his daughter at all.

The letter was written by a very sick man. During the course of the investigation, I never met him. I have pictures of him, and I now know some of the things he did, but just reading this letter, he was short of being insane. He would say, "I love you," and then go into a rage, cussing at her, using every fowl word imaginable, then back to "I love you" again.

I almost felt sorry for Penny; because I knew that she was totally controlled by her husband and was a victim of very severe abuse at his hands, based on what he wrote.

I then drove to the flea market where Penny was supposed to sell her brass pieces and discovered that the pieces were sold there before the fire, not after. I interviewed as many people as possible who had seen some of the items she was selling. One was another brass dealer, and she was upset because Penny was selling the items at about half their value and she did not sell anything the entire weekend that Penny was there.

Based on the fact that we had an arson fire, the letter from the sheriff's department, and the statement that I took from the insured, which was full of holes, we were just about ready to deny the claim, but I was not comfortable in doing this yet.

I had the insured selling brass items from her shop before the fire, she was behind in her mortgage payments, and her business was in the toilet.

I still didn't think I had enough to deny the claim in this state. It was not a jury-friendly insurance state.

Sometimes you had to weigh your case against a bad jury, and most of the time I was not going to put my company's money on the line unless I had at least an 80 percent chance of winning in front of a jury. I was at about 60 percent at this point, and I still had to maintain the innocence of the insured in my mind until the scale weighed the other way against her. Right now it was about 40 percent for her and 60 percent for us on the teeter-totter.

I was in my office working on other cases one afternoon when I received the call that would blow this case wide open. It was from the principal of the grade school where the little Johnson girl attended school. Let's call her Ann.

The principal told me that he had Ann in his office—she had my business card in her hand, and she made him call me. He said he didn't know what it was about, but she was insistent that he call me right away and would not leave his office until I got there. He told her he should probably call her parents, and she refused to let him do this.

He probably thought I was some kind of a child predator until I told him that I was working on her mother's fire claim and I would be there as soon as I could.

I told the principal to call the sheriff's office and ask for the juvenile officer and have her come and stay with the little girl until I got there. I made a three-hour drive in record time.

I arrived at the school and had a very lengthy discussion about the situation with the sheriff's juvenile officer and the principal.

I asked Ann if this was in regard to the fire, and she said yes. She said she wanted to tell me everything, but she could not go back home or her parents would beat her severely.

I had the juvenile officer call the juvenile judge and explain everything that was happening. He ordered temporary custody of the child to the juvenile officer and the principal.

I got out my recorder and asked her if it was okay if I recorded the conversation. She agreed, and both the sheriff and the principle were present.

I called our company attorney and made sure that everything I had done and was doing was legal; so as to further protect the company and myself. The attorney gave me the green light.

I first asked Ann how she had obtained my business card and why she had called for me.

She said that when her mother wasn't looking, she put the card into her pocket and hid it. She said that the reason she called me was because I seemed like I cared and I was nice to her. She said it was like I laid my card on the desk so she would pick it up.

I then asked her to just tell us everything.

She didn't start talking about the fire, and I saw the deputies eyes begin to tear as she told her story. Then the tears turned to rage against this child's parents.

Ann said that her parents were really bad people and they had staged many fake accidents and made her be a part of them. She said that her entire family was involved—cousins, uncles, aunts, her grandmother, and her mother and father. She named about ten people.

She had very detailed information about dates, times, and places and exactly what had occurred.

Her story went like this:

The family would meet at a hotel—usually they would get two rooms—and they would either have junk cars that they bought off car lots or they would have rental cars.

They would take out insurance on the cars with an agent that was out of their hometown area and ask for the highest coverage they could get.

If it was a rental car, they would take out the maximum allowable coverage for everything.

They never even had to pay any premiums on the insurance because they said they would mail it in to the companies, and their coverage was bound and policies issued.

Her dad was the leader. He would plan everything, and he was ruthless. She did say that he was very fair about the money split, but no one should ever cross him because the consequence would be fatal.

They would meet in the hotel room for hours, planning where the accident would occur, what they would say to the police when they arrived, and what would be said to the insurance agents and the insurance adjusters.

If they saw any problem whatsoever, they would tell the adjusters that they were turning over their claims to their attorney, and the bad-guy attorney would step in and start the threats of a lawsuit and punitive damages.

They would then pick out the drivers and passengers of each car, making sure that they had never used the same combination before to throw off suspicion. She said that sometimes the attorneys were at the hotel to make sure that everything went right.

She said that was when the bad things started happening, after all the plans were made.

The drivers would be issued crash helmets so they really wouldn't get hurt, and the passengers would be transported to the scene in another car after the actual impact of the cars.

She said that her dad would then take a razor blade to one of the passenger's foreheads and slice open a gaping cut, and it would be bleeding very badly.

He would take his fist and break several of their noses; he would break fingers and toes so they actually would have injuries. She went on and on about the things that her dad would do to her relatives, and we had to stop many times because she would break down crying and have to get her composure.

Then she laid the bomb on us. She said that her own dad would make her hold her arm out straight, and he would break it. She said the pain was unbearable, and sometimes she would have to be in this pain for hours until the accident was staged, they were transported to the accident scene, and the passengers brought in and placed methodically in their positions.

She said that she knew of a pair of glasses that they used about twenty times, which were already broken, and also false teeth that were broken, which they used on every accident for her mother because she had no teeth.

The thing about all of the medical bills, the glasses, and the false teeth is that when an adjuster is figuring up what a bodily injury claim is worth, you take the bottom line figure and then multiply that figure by three, and that is what they get. If an attorney is involved, the figure usually increases to four or five times just to get rid of it.

Whatever settlement the drivers and passengers received, the attorney would usually get a third of the total paid claim.

She said that her dad broke both of her arms twice each, and she was in casts for many months over the last several years, and the principal verified this.

Her statement regarding the insurance fraud accident claims was enough for me to call the FBI and tell the agent that had contacted me that I had just discovered a goldmine for him. He was there in less than an hour.

The amazing thing was that I really felt good about busting this insurance fraud ring, but it didn't help me with my fire claim.

I almost felt guilty when I asked her about the fire. She had been through enough already, but I was glad that I did.

She said that on the night of the fire, she and her mother stopped at a gas station, at the direction of her father, who was in jail. She said they bought gasoline, and her father had told her mother how much, where to pour the gasoline, and what to use to start it with. She said that they went upstairs first and poured gas then went downstairs and poured some more all over, but she remembered her mother saying that they had to get out quick so the fumes wouldn't build up inside.

Her dad knew what he was talking about. I have seen many an arsonists in the hospital because they waited too long after they poured the gas to actually light the fire. It is the fumes that burn and explode, not the actual gas itself.

Ann said her mother even broke out a window to make it look like someone broke in.

The day before the fire, she had to help her mother remove a lot of the inventory from the building so they could sell it at a flea market, claim the entire inventory was destroyed in the fire, and hope that the adjuster would be stupid.

She said that her father directed this entire fire from his jail cell, talking to his wife on the phone and sending her letters.

The end result of this little girl's testimony was that the parents were arrested and charged with arson. They were also arrested and charged on many counts of insurance fraud for the accidents, and as far as I know, they are still in jail.

The FBI loved me, the sheriff's department and arson investigator loved me, my company loved me, but none of the praise compared to this one fact.

I have been in this job for thirty-four years. I have seen just about everything. I have been threatened and had contracts out on me. I have backed down people that had guns on me when I interviewed them, but at the same time letting them know that I had a .38 special pointed at their groin underneath the table. I have handled million-dollar cases and busted them. I have testified at a murder trial where I sent two guys to the electric chair, but nothing in my entire career has even come close to this case.

By leaving one business card at a fire scene, I got Ann out of that horrible situation; got her taken away from these devil parents, and the last I heard she was growing up with a nice, caring, Christian family.

I never heard what happened to her after that day. If she is reading this book— she is probably about thirty years old now—I wish she would contact me. She knows who she is if she reads this book, and I would just like to know how she is doing.

If I never defeat another fraud case in my entire career, nothing will ever even come close to this one in the gratification I have felt over all these years for Ann. Remember, this entire story was because of one business card.

BUSINESS CARD NUMBER TWO

This next case was also solved by the use of a business card. It is one of the most bizarre cases I have worked, and at the end of this chapter I think you will agree.

This case began with me receiving the assignment of a death, let's say, in Louisiana. We insured a roofing contractor, and we carried not only all of his liability insurance but also his workers comp coverage.

He carried a high single-person death benefit of $350,000 cash for an on-the-job fatality.

The adjuster called me and said that this one was not going to be fun. The employee that the death claim was for was actually the insured's son. The insured we will call Henry, and his son was Josh. Josh was married, and the case had a lot of publicity. The agent was also going to be a problem, because he had been a very close friend of the entire family and Henry was his best friend.

I asked the adjuster why he even wanted me to become involved. He said that he had received two anonymous tips from hang-up phone calls telling him that he should look at this claim very closely and that it was not what it appeared to be. He said he thought it may have been the same person. I asked the adjuster if he had caller ID, and he said his was broken. I told him to go out and get another one immediately.

I reviewed the claim file, and it appeared to be pretty plain and simple. Henry's son, Josh, had been working on a roof with his crew, and he fell off. Josh went home after being checked out by the ambulance crew and took the rest of the day off. He then disappeared from his home and was found in the woods about two miles from his home. He had fallen into a snake pit full of rattlers, had about thirty snake bites on his body, and was dead.

The coroner's report stated that he did an autopsy and found a brain aneurism. His theory was that the fall caused brain damage. After Josh had been home for a while, he became delirious and didn't know what he was doing, walked into the woods, and when the aneurism hit him, it killed him immediately.

The coroner stated that the death was from the fall and not the snake bites. He observed that the son was dead before he even hit the ground.

Henry, father of the deceased, was filing a claim on behalf of his son's wife for the workers comp claim of $350,000.

I want to warn you that in the end of this story you may be upset that the end result, thinking that insurance policies are wrong for the exclusions they have in them, and this claim, in your opinion, should probably have been paid.

I find this dilemma very often in my investigations. Sometimes the policies can be ambiguous and they do sometimes seem unfair.

You must remember one thing, though: I work for the insurance company, and insurance companies are guided by the written contract between the insured and the company that wrote the policy. When an insured buys a policy, he should read the policy to see what it covers and what it does not. It is usually pretty black and white, except when attorneys get involved and try to change the wording and the intent of the policy to have their client's claim covered, even though the insurance company never intended to cover the situation that occurred that the attorney or the insured is trying to have covered.

Any claim that I get involved in; I have the insured sign a non-waiver form before I start the investigation. This form advises the insured that the claim will be handled exactly by the verbiage of the policy, the company has to do anything they agreed to do in the policy, as does the insured, and neither is waiving any of its rights under the policy. What this means is that you bought a policy and we will handle your claim based on what is covered and what is not covered, and if it is not covered, we will not pay your claim.

This is very hard for a lot of people to understand, and I sympathize with them. A lot of times it does appear to be unfair.

I am okay with this, and I have seen adjusters and my own company stretch the policy to the limits to see if they can cover a claim that really had no coverage for in the contract.

The exception to this feeling of mine that the policy should be stretched every now and then is when the insured lies or commits fraud to get the claim covered, and that is what occurred in this claim.

I drove to Louisiana the next day and started my investigation. I first went to the agency, and I started getting a bad feeling right away. You have to remember one thing: most of our agents are really good people. They are independent agents and usually write their clients' policies with three or four different insurance companies. If they choose my company to write the coverage, then we accept the premium, and the agent usually gets about 10 to 15 percent of the total amount, and we agree to handle any losses during the policy period from inception to expiration.

As I said, most agents are very honest people, but some are real dirt balls. They lie about the claims, they back-date coverage's, and sometimes even pocket the premium, write fake policies, and give the insured a policy they made up. They never contact us about the policy, even though our name is on the policy. The agent just hopes that the insured never has any losses and he pockets $1,000, $2,000, or even more, depending on the type and size of the policy. Some commercial policies could put $50,000 into the agent's pocket, and if the business has no losses, at the end of the policy period he breathes a sigh of relief and puts the $50,000 into his checking account. This is insurance fraud, and we have put many agents in jail for this and recovered our money in many different ways, even to the point of taking over the agency.

The thing that most people do not know is that in some states, even though we never had a policy and we never received any premium for the policy, this would be a fake certificate of insurance that gives coverage to, say, a roofer who is required to show insurance to get a job with a larger contractor. Many times these fake certificates are purchased at seminars for $100 and that could save them $20,000 if they actually bought a policy. If we do not put a stop to it after we are made aware of the fake policy, then we may have to pay for any losses sustained due to the fake policy.

In this claim I got a bad feeling after the short interview with the agent. I did not get the impression that there was any premium problem, but I got the feeling that the agent knew something he was not telling me.

I usually have to be very careful with agents and what I say to them. The politics are very real, and this agent may be a personal friend of someone in the company I work for. Sometimes you walk on eggshells until you have enough evidence that it wouldn't make any difference what I do, the agent will go to jail.

After I left the agent's office, I went to the local police department that handled the investigation. I did not get a friendly reception there, and everyone was very standoffish.

Normally when I introduce myself as a former police officer, I get great cooperation and they cannot do enough to assist me.

In this case all I got was the coroner's report, and the police said, "The coroner's report says it all!"

I then went to the coroner, and I thought that I had killed this guy's dog from the attitude I got when I first introduced myself.

First he said he didn't have time to speak with me and I would have to come back in about three hours.

When I went back and finally got to speak with him, he was very curt. He wanted to know why I was even investigating the claim. He knew what occurred and asked why I was putting the family through this investigation ordeal just after they had buried their son and his wife had buried a husband. He accused me of having no sympathy for the family in any way.

I tried to explain to the doctor that I was just doing my job, but he didn't care.

He showed me the autopsy photos, and they were really gross. I had been through several autopsies before when I was a state cop, but none were like this one. The body had been found in a swamp in the woods two days after Josh was missing. The temperature was about 95 degrees, and he had been bitten about thirty times by rattlesnakes. His body was swollen twice the size that it normally was, and it had turned black.

The autopsy photos were in various stages of the actual autopsy.

Again, I am no stranger to this, and I know how it is done. First, an incision is made under the neck and around to each earlobe. The incision goes just skin deep and the coroner then takes the skin, lifts it up, and folds the entire face up and over the top of the skull, and it just sort of hangs there. The skull is then cut with a saw, the brain removed and checked for any injury, and hopefully the cause of death is discovered.

When the cause has been found and documented, the skull is replaced and the skin that was folded back is pulled back down onto the front of the face, and *voila,* you are back where you started. After a few stitches, you would never know what just occurred. It is not for the weak stomach. I have had several young troopers with me that had to leave and vomit after their first one.

The coroner showed me photos of a bloody mass in the brain that he said was the cause of death.

I asked him how he could be so sure, and this really upset him.

I also asked him about the drug screen. He really got upset this time and said that a drug screen had not been done. I asked him if any type of blood had been drawn before the body was taken to the funeral home, and he said none had been taken.

I asked him why, and this was my big mistake.

He told me to leave his office immediately and he had nothing else to say to me. I had insulted him and his professional competency, and I had no idea what I was talking about. He was the doctor and the coroner, and I was nothing.

I left his office.

I called the insured, Henry, and asked if I could set up interviews with his employees. He at first objected to this and said it was not necessary. He said that the coroner had already ruled on the death and asked why I was doing an investigation.

I told Henry that he didn't have any choice. I was very sorry for his loss, but I had to interview all of the employees that worked with his son. He said that there were three crews his son supervised, and that would be about thirty people. I told him that I would take two days if I had to complete the interviews.

He said he would check with his attorney. He finally called me back and stated that he would allow the interviews of his employees, but his attorney would have to be there and represent all of his employees.

I simply asked Henry, "Why?"

He became very angry with this and said that he had his daughter-in-law's best interests at heart and he didn't want us to trick his employees into saying something that would allow us to get out of paying his son's claim.

I agreed to the attorney being present and told Henry we would start the next morning.

For the next day and a half, I interviewed thirty employees. It was like interviewing zombies that had a tape recorder of what they were supposed to say.

After about the fifteenth employee, I looked over at Henry's attorney and laughed. This was getting ridiculous. They all said the same thing, and it was scripted.

I told the attorney that this was really unusual for everyone to have the same story and answers to my questions. He didn't say anything.

Every employee would not even look at me. They kept their heads down to the floor, or every once in a while they would look at the attorney.

I gave every one of them my business card, and I had written on the card where I was staying in town and the room number. About half of them left the card where it laid on the desk.

Some of them actually laid the card beside me when they left, but I noticed one employee put the business card into his pocket.

I thought this was interesting, and I could only hope that I had hit pay dirt on this one. Was he the caller that would not identify himself to our adjuster?

The scripted story coming from thirty employees was that Henry's son, Josh, was the salt of the earth. He was a great family man, didn't drink, smoke, or use any type of drug. He loved his wife and kids and was a great boss. He treated every employee fairly and was a very hard worker.

On the day of the fall, Josh was on the roof, slipped off, and hit his head when he fell. He just didn't seem right, and he was driven home by another coworker.

The next thing they knew, they had heard that he had died as a result of the fall damaging his brain.

When I had finished with all of the employees, I got Henry's attorney to the side and made a casual remark to him. "It seems as though everyone that was here today went to school and was told what to say."

He became very agitated with my comment and told me he was going to file a formal complaint against me with my supervisors.

I remember going back to my hotel and calling my wife. I told her that night that if my hunches were wrong, I could be in a lot of trouble on this one with my company and my boss.

My boss, Phil, has always given me enough rope to hang myself and pretty much left me alone. I have never done anything to get the company in trouble in my thirty-four years with them, and I thought that this might be the first time that he would be very disappointed in me.

I went to my room and waited—six o'clock, seven o'clock, nothing. Then it happened. At eight o'clock I got the call.

It was from the one employee who had taken my card and put in his pocket.

He asked me if he could come speak with me. He said something was really bothering him and he had to get it off of his chest.

I told him that the bar in the hotel was pretty empty and I could meet with him there. He arrived, and we found a quiet corner. I had my tape recorder running.

I did not do this to trap him in any way; I did it to protect myself. I wanted the recorder to show that from the time I met with him, I had promised him nothing and had not put words in his mouth.

After the first contact with him, I asked him if he wanted a drink. He said a Cuba Libre—this was great, and I really liked this guy right off, because that was also what I drank. During the course of the conversation, we had two each.

After I developed a rapport with him, I asked him if I could record the conversation. He agreed, but with the stipulation that his name never be used. He said if they knew who came forward, he would lose his job, and he had a wife and two kids.

I always promise the same thing to informants like this, that I will protect their identity as long as I can, but if a judge would ever tell me that I have to give up their name or go to jail, I would have to give up his name at that time. Until then he would be protected.

He agreed to this, and I brought out the recorder, already running.

I did the introductions, and then he told me a story that blew me away.

He said that he had worked for the company for about five years. He knew Josh well and said he was a really bad dude. He said that Josh was hooked up on cocaine and would use it at work almost every day. Most of the time when he got high, they would try to keep him off the roof of a job so he would not get hurt.

He said on the day of the fall, the insured's son had climbed up on the roof after taking several hits in his car. He said he was totally stoned and he saw him use the drugs. They tried to keep him off the roof, but he fought them. He said that the son went up on the roof, stood on the peak, and said, "Watch me. I am Superman!" and he jumped off the roof, thinking he could fly.

He said he hit the ground hard then got up, and they went to him immediately to see if he was okay. He said he was okay, but he thought he better go home. He also told me that one of the other guys went by to check on Josh and caught him using cocaine again. That was the last time they saw him.

The next thing they knew, he was dead after being missing for several days.

He said the worst thing was that Henry had called all of them together after I left the first day. He told them that they all had to come in and give statements the next day. He said that all of them would be required to come in that night and attend a meeting with his attorney on what they were supposed to say to me.

They all came in and they had a school on what they could say and what they could not say. They were instructed not to say anything about the cocaine use or how the fall really occurred.

He said that this really bothered all of the employees, but they were told if they did not do this, they would lose their job—but worse than that, the wife and kids of the insured's son would not get any money from the insurance company.

The attorney told all the employees that if the insurance company could show drug use on the job, that the claim would be excluded.

He also said that the doctor covered up the drug usage by not taking any blood and running any tests on the son.

At the end of the interview, I thanked him for coming forward. I told him I knew this had to be hard for him to do what he did. He said it was probably the hardest thing he had ever done in his life, but he just couldn't live with himself for telling the lie to me when I interviewed him.

I figure one out of thirty honest people was hard to believe, but that is the case with a lot of investigations I do.

Again, insurance companies do not get a lot of cooperation from anyone, mainly due to the fact that people think insurance companies rip everyone off every chance that they get. I admit I have seen some companies that were like this, and instead of looking for a way to pay a claim, they look for a way to deny a claim.

I always try to look for a way to pay a claim, every time. But when the investigation shows otherwise, I will go to trial on a $5,000 claim, even though it may cost us $10,000 to defend it.

The next morning I called the insured's attorney and told him just one thing.

I said, "I have an informant that came forward. I know about drug usage. I know about the doctor. I know about the meeting you had with all of the employees and what you told them to say."

I then told him that I expected him to report to his client, let him know what I said, and I wanted him to call me the next day and advise me if they wanted to proceed with their claim or withdraw the claim.

He had nothing to say other than, "I will call you tomorrow."

Within a half hour my phone rang and the attorney told me they wished to withdraw their claim.

I met with him, drew up the paperwork, and the claim ended.

I am so glad that it did end that way. The publicity would have been terrible, the court case would have been long, and I would probably have had to give up my informant at some point. The doctor would probably have lost his license, the attorney would probably have lost his license, and Henry would probably have been charged with insurance fraud.

At the start of this chapter I told you there were some claims that really bother me when I have to go by the wording of the contract, but in this case it had to be done. Do I still feel sorry for the wife? Yes. Do I feel sorry about having to have forced a withdrawal of this claim? Yes, but that is my job. What is the old expression? It is a dirty job, but someone has to do it.

THE CIVIL WAR ARTIST

This next chapter is about a very weird story that takes investigation, punitive damages, and high dollar amounts to the edge.

I can tell you the entire story except for the final outcome. This claim was compromised on the courthouse steps. We did a full investigation, and the way it ended up will surprise you. The final amount that my company agreed to pay will not be divulged due to an agreement between the insured's attorney and ours, but the payment was very minimal as opposed to what the demand was.

The claim started out in a small town that was close to an air force base in an eastern state. The insured was an Iranian. There is really no reason to tell you this other than some of the things that transpired because of his being an Iranian.

The insured had been in the service for several years but had eventually gotten out and settled down in this small town. He was a mediocre artist and had a great interest in the Civil War.

I will give him credit for his tenacity in his field. He would go to the battle scenes and do a complete study of the scene before he would pick his next subject to paint.

Let's call the insured John. He had changed his birth name to an American name after he joined the Air Force.

John was divorced and had several children by his first wife. John lived at his studio, and sometimes his girlfriend would stay at the studio, but she had her own home. The studio was situated downtown in this small city. It was an eastern town, so I imagine John had a lot of prejudice to overcome, even though he had served in our armed forces for six years.

I must admit one thing: I really got to know John well, and I really liked him. We got along great, even though we sat through interviews, countless meetings, his examination under oath, my deposition, and then his deposition just prior to going to a jury trial.

I probably worked on this claim longer than any other claim I have ever had. The hours I spent on this were unbelievable but necessary. Every time I worked on this claim, I would have to drive four hours just to get there and then start whatever investigation needed to be done at that time.

I also met an attorney that I have developed a lifelong friendship with as a result of this claim. Earlier I said I could count on one hand the number of really good attorneys that I have respect for. Our attorney in this claim is one of them. To not totally embarrass him I will just call him Drew.

Drew is a true gentleman. He is the most thorough attorney I have ever worked with, and his demand for excellence and detail is unbelievable.

John had a very large office space that used to be some type of a warehouse. It had huge steel beams in the rear and, the good thing for my investigation, only two entrances to the building. There was one door in the rear and one in the front. The insured had converted the front area into a gallery where he displayed his artwork, and in the rear portion he had built a pretty nice living area. The rest of the warehouse was storage for all of his prints, and he had thousands. He thought that he could compete with other Civil War artists that have made it really big in the industry. One of the more famous artists I actually used as an expert witness in the investigation of this fire. I got to know John, and his heart was in his paintings, but his paintings were not selling.

About two months before his huge fire, he increased his insurance coverage from $500,000 to 2.5 million dollars. During the investigation I found out that there was no reason for this, and he had the same inventory when he took out the additional coverage that he had before he took it out. Had his paintings increased in value this much?

No. The bottom line was that he was having a fire sale and my company was the buyer, so he thought.

I got the call on the large fire. The first thing I do when I get a large loss like this is check with underwriting and see if there has been an increase in coverage within the last six months. This is a pretty good red flag if I am going to have a questionable claim. You notice I said questionable; I cannot say fraud or arson at this point in the investigation. Remember, I always give the insured the benefit of the doubt until I prove otherwise.

I discovered that John had increased his coverage from the $500,000 to the 2.5 million, and the worst thing about it was that underwriting had done this without asking any questions at all. I asked them why they did this and could get no explanation.

I learned one thing a long time ago: I take a claim as I get it. Anything that has been done prior to this is past history, and there is nothing I can do about it. The company makes mistakes, agents make mistakes, our adjusters make mistakes, and sometimes it is my job to clean up messes and proceed with the investigation.

Sometimes I cannot clean them up, so I just tell the adjuster that they screwed up and tell them to pay the claim no matter how much it is, because they did something that would put the company in bad faith, and this could cost us big time.

This claim started out with a bad situation from the first e-mail I received from the adjuster reporting the claim.

The e-mail read, "Jack, I have a new fire loss. It will probably be about $2 million, and the insured is an Iranian."

Okay, put yourself on a jury, and you are debating if my company had a prejudice against the insured from day one. Then have John's attorney put this e-mail on a six-foot-by-six-foot screen in the courtroom then asks the adjuster, "Why did you say this in your e-mail?"

It has nothing to do with the claim. I don't care if the insured is white, red, yellow brown, or black, or what his nationality is; I treat them all the same. I gather the facts of the claim and let the chips fall where they may.

I don't manufacture evidence, and I don't lie about anything. If the investigation shows that the insured should be paid, he gets paid; if it doesn't, then he does not get paid.

I asked the adjuster why he put this into the e-mail, and he said he wasn't thinking correctly and he knew now that he shouldn't have.

Sometimes I can salvage something like this, and on this one I felt that the stakes were high enough that I needed to do something right away.

I sent an e-mail to the adjuster, his supervisor, and the home office supervisor. I just said that he should not have used the word *Iranian* and it didn't matter what race or country the person was from. I told him that he would never do this again and we would handle the investigation with an open mind from this point on.

Just so you know how huge this was, later on in the claim investigation, this adjuster was in his deposition concerning this claim. He was questioned for three hours on that one sentence. It was not pretty, and he was sweating bullets by the time he insured's attorney got through with him.

I got this cleared up and drove to the city where the claim occurred.

I first went to the fire department, and they said they needed some help right away. They had a huge problem with the soundness of the structure. They needed a crane to come in and support a wall and a backhoe to remove debris so they could determine what caused this fire. The arson investigator told me that he had never seen a fire that burned this hot, and they suspected arson as soon as they arrived. The most important part of an arson investigation is to check if there is forcible entry.

I always see if there is forcible entry, and if there is not, I look to the insured to explain to me how someone could have entered their building. I ask who all had keys to the building or home, and then I start from there eliminating people. If I come down to the final stages and the insured had the only key or access that night, this is great evidence against the insured and their story of how the fire started.

I also have to rule out all other causes of the fire. As soon as I started looking around at the scene, I knew I had a problem. The steel beams that supported the structure were bent. This takes a very high temperature to do this—usually arson caused by a lot of accelerant being poured in the right places.

I immediately called in my own cause-and-origin investigator to do a separate investigation from the fire department, but he would work alongside the fire department investigator.

The city did not have the funds to rent the crane and backhoe, so I approved the rental of these two pieces of equipment and the operators as long as the city needed them.

In exchange for this, I asked that every care be taken to preserve the integrity of the rear door of the building. The reason for this is that the front door was found to be locked when the fire department arrived and they had to force the door open. The rear of the building had already collapsed when they got there, and I needed that door lock to check to see if it was forced or unlocked.

I first met John at the fire scene, and he appeared to be a little nervous, but one thing was missing. He was not upset, he was not mad; he was not devastated at losing his entire life's work with all of his prints ruined. This was not normal, and when I see abnormal reactions in an insured, the red flags start to fly.

We started digging, and this continued for two days. There were several times that we thought a wall was going to collapse on us and had to move the crane around to protect the firefighters and the arson investigators.

When we eventually did get the scene fairly cleared away, we found multiple points of origin where an accelerant had been used. Samples were taken and sent to the lab for analysis.

Great care was also taken to rule out every possible electrical failure, because the fire department said the insured commented that his lights had been blinking off and on prior to the fire, and this was what he thought the cause of the fire was. Every light fixture was checked and re-checked for failure, and none was found. The outlets also showed no shorts of any kind. We searched for every extension cord that the insured had, and these also did not fail. Every appliance in the building was also checked for failure, and we had none. The insured and his girlfriend did smoke, and this was also checked out. This was ruled out because I had six points of origin. Careless smoking would only reveal one point of origin, and it would be a slow-burning fire. This was a very rapid, accelerated fire.

It was also very interesting that the worst burn area in the entire building was around the prints that the insured had, and there were thousands of them. The intent was obviously to burn up the prints, but they were so compressed in their boxes in stacks that a lot of them were burned, but most were just smoke damaged. It really didn't matter; their resale value was now nothing, due to the smoke damage and edges of the prints being scorched.

I knew right away based on what I knew of the costs of Civil War prints, I probably had a total loss fire of $2.5 million. I knew that I had a huge task ahead of me and would spend a lot of time on this investigation.

After the fire was determined to be arson, many photos were taken, and samples were sent to the lab, I started looking for the rear door. This was finally found in a pile of debris. The door lock was intact, but the door totally burned away except for the frame. The lock was found to be in the locked position with the deadbolt set. This was photographed and taken into evidence.

I then started looking around the living area where John resided with his children and his girlfriend, Beth. The children were only there occasionally due to John's ex-wife having full custody.

I always look for things that are there and things that are not there. If someone burns their home or building, they will usually mess up and take with them things that they do not want to burn up in the fire.

In this fire, I noticed that the pantry was almost empty and clothing was very sparse. The refrigerator had very few items in it, and the freezer was almost empty. Most people do not think that we will look for these items. They do not fill up the freezer with meat the week before they plan to burn their building or home down.

A lot of people will also go to garage sales and replace their clothing with garage-sale items and take their good clothing to a storage facility.

I also look for family photos that are not replaceable and for items that people normally have out for display, like knickknacks and family Bibles, etc.

Remember the family Bible; it played a huge part in this investigation. I also look for firearms, which, no matter how hot the fire, will still be intact. I also ask about cash. Almost everyone has a cash stash in their home somewhere. This could range from fifty dollars to five thousand dollars, but almost everyone has this. I always ask where these items were, and then I start looking for them.

In this case, when I finally interviewed John, the two things that he said were in the fire that were most precious to him were a Bible his father had given him and his .38 revolver that he kept for protection.

The insured, I later found, professed to be a very devout Christian. The problem the insured had with the Bible was that I hired what is called a sifter to come to the fire scene. The insured had told me that the items were in his family living area, and after the sift of an area that was probably burned the least, these two items could not be found.

This was a huge red flag in the claim and was later one of the reasons for the denial of John's claim.

The examination of the fire scene was pretty dangerous. The walls were unsteady, the steel supports were cracking and making noises like they would collapse at any time, and all of the time the building sounded like it was coming down, we were underneath all of this digging out the fire scene.

It was very unusual to have a fire department and arson investigator that were as cooperative as the ones in this city. The conclusion of the investigation of the scene was jointly agreed to; it was arson, and John was the prime suspect.

John was cooperative to start with and gave me an interview.

He stated that on the night of the fire, he and his family had taken a trip out of town and visited some relatives about an hour away.

The bad thing for John was that after I applied a timeline on the time the fire started, fire department arrived, etc.; John could have been at the scene of the fire right before he left for his relatives' house.

I did confirm that he got there, but there was no definite time period showing that he was there at the time the fire started. He could have set the fire, left town, and then arrived at his relatives' house.

I usually don't get very concerned even if the insured does have an airtight alibi. Our policy says that we can deny a claim for arson if we have three things present.

1. An accelerated or set fire

2. A motive

3. The opportunity to have set the fire or have someone else set the fire

As you can see, number three is pretty much wide open and left to interpretation. All you have to do is be able to show that the insured set the fire or he might have possibly hired someone to set the fire, and if you have the other two items present, you could possibly deny the fire claim and the entire payment.

In this case, I will explain later, the financial motive was very evident.

In John's interview, I discovered that he was in financial trouble, his prints were not selling like they should, and his alimony was killing him.

He was emphatic about not having anything to do with setting the fire and said that he and his girlfriend, Beth, had been receiving what he thought were death threats.

He said that he had been receiving hate mail because of his nationality and his girlfriend had been finding Barbie dolls in her car, outside of her apartment, at her work place, etc. The Barbie dolls were cut up, with nooses around their necks, painted with what looked like blood, and had their heads cut off and bloody substances poured over where the neck would have been. The thing about Beth was that she looked like a Barbie doll, and John's ex-wife, Joan, referred to her as Barbie. It was John's thoughts, when he told me all this, that Joan hated Beth and had set the fire.

The most bizarre thing about this was that during the investigation I could not prove it 100 percent, but I was about 90 percent sure that the John and Beth had actually planted all of the Barbie dolls to make it look as though Joan was involved in the fire.

I noticed one thing about John that also became very interesting later in the investigation. He carried in his pocket a box opener attached to a key ring.

About one week into the investigation, when I was starting to ask John a lot of questions about the fire, his Bible, his gun, where he was at when the fire started, his business etc, there was a reported attempted rape and cutting of Beth.

Someone apparently broke through a window and used a knife to make her take her clothes off and cut her many times with what appeared to be a box opener. This occurred at Beth's home where she lived primarily; the rest of the time she would stay over at John's apartment. The cuts were very minor, but they were placed in certain spots over her body.

If you are thinking what you should right now as a remote investigator, you are right. The cuts on her body matched up with the cuts on the Barbie dolls that had been left at various locations. Coincidence?

Oh, and she was not actually raped. The person who broke into her apartment tried to have sex with her, but according to Beth's statement to the police, he could not get an erection and he fled the scene. She said that she fought dramatically with him. The only problem with this story is that her two children (from her first marriage) were asleep in the next bedroom, and they didn't even wake up with all this noise going on, slamming into walls, things breaking in the room, and a knock-down, drag-out fight, according to the girlfriend.

It was obvious to me that John and Beth was doing everything they could to make it look like someone was out to get him and set the fire to his building.

I again asked John why he had increased his coverage just a few weeks before the fire. He said that he had a publisher that was going to really start pushing his paintings and he knew that their value would increase dramatically and he was afraid that the old building might catch fire.

I asked him the name of the publishing company, and he said that all of those records burned up in the fire.

I also asked him for tax records, and this was another red flag. He said everything he had as far as sales records and IRS statements had burned up in the fire.

This was also interesting because I then found out that the IRS had sent him a three-year audit request for the last three years, two weeks before the fire.

Are you now starting to get just a little bit suspicious?

Many times I have had fires that were not set to destroy the building, they were fires that were set to destroy records after an IRS request for audit.

Fires are also set to destroy inventory; I call these fire sales to the insurance company.

This claim had both.

John advised that he had over $60,000 in credit card debt, that he owed the printer of his paintings a lot of money—about $200,000—and many other debts were owed.

I felt sorry for John. He was a nice guy. I really did like him, and we got along well.

I told you earlier that I do not judge people and I just let the chips fall as they do on any investigation.

In addition to interviewing John and Beth, I also interviewed the ex-wife, Joan, and her boyfriend. They were very interesting people. They all lived in a very small house, but it was very clean. Joan told me that there was no doubt in her mind that John had set the fire, and on top of that, he was one sick dude. She said that he professed to be a Christian and carried his Bible around all of the time, but he was a sexual deviant and that was why she divorced him.

She said that her children would come home from the required visits at John's gallery/home and they said that he walked around the house naked and he and Beth actually had sex in front of them and they watched.

I asked Joan if she would allow me to interview her children, and she said yes. I got a recorded statement from all of them, and they admitted to me that this happened.

I met with the authorities the next day, and when they went to interview the children, they totally changed their stories and said that this never happened and they had lied to me.

I discovered later that John heard about the interview from his children and he bought the children extravagant gifts to change their stories.

So I had a set fire, I had a financial motive, and I had John not being able to really establish an alibi. Then I had some really bizarre things going on that were very unusual. I also could not find the Bible or the gun that was in the building.

I hired an attorney, and we decided to ask John to come in for an examination under oath, which is something that is usually done pre-denial of a claim. If the insured can answer all of the questions we have, then his claim will probably be paid. If he cannot, then the claim will probably be denied. If he lies, the claim will be denied.

John was told that he did have the right to have an attorney present, and he hired a very good one. I still wonder why the attorney took the case, because John had no money.

Just before the insured was advised of his examination under oath request and before getting an attorney, I received a call from Joan, and she asked me, "Did he claim his Bible was stolen or burned up in the fire?" I told her he had. She said that she had seen him with his Bible when she dropped off the kids for their required custody visit with him. She said she would help me in any way that she could so he would go to jail and she wouldn't have to send her kids to him anymore.

I did a cold call on John the next day, using the excuse I was there to see if he had any of the documents I had requested.

I noticed that he had a Bible with him. The one that he had described as being burned in the fire was supposed to be signed by his father. I asked him if I could see the Bible, and he refused.

The next time I saw him he showed me a Bible, but it was not the same one that he had that day. Another huge red flag.

In the examination under oath of John, he was asked many questions about the fire, his prints, etc. He said that his prints were just starting to become popular and they had a good market developing. He said that before the fire, a man had come into his shop and offered him $10,000 for his one painting. The fire occurred before he could sell it to him, and it was ruined in the fire. Of course, he didn't have this man's name or any information about him.

I had been working with the police, and it was also interesting that I knew they had asked John to take a polygraph because they thought that he set the fire but they could not prove it.

I knew that John had refused the test. During the exam, he was asked if the police had asked him to take a polygraph, and he said no. We asked him if they did ask him would he take it, and he said that he would. Later the police asked him again, and he refused it again.

After the EUO, my attorney wanted me to tie up the loose end of the door. We had the rear door locked, but we wanted to make sure that the fire department saw the rear door intact when they were fighting the fire and also to get statements that they had busted in the front door when they arrived. I got statements from all of the firefighters that were there that night, and the general consensus was that the rear door was intact but it was too dangerous to try to gain entry through it. They all said that the front door was closed and locked when they arrived and they had to break it in. They fought the fire from the front door to the rear of the building, and when they got to the middle, they said that the fire was so intense that they had to leave the building and just let it burn.

I asked all of them if they had ever seen a fire this hot, and they all said no. There was no doubt in their mind that it was a set fire.

We eventually denied the claim, and then the fun began. We took the deposition of John, and then he and his attorney took the depositions of me, our adjuster, and the home office supervisor.

This was the point that the adjuster wished he had never made the statement, "The insured is an Iranian." This is where he was browbeaten for three hours on that one statement. He was very drained at the end of the deposition.

The home office supervisor was next, and he just went over the investigation as it had been reported to him and why he had made the decision to deny the claim. You will note that I said "he" denied the claim. This is a very useful tool in our company setup. I investigate the claim and turn over my findings to the home office supervisor, who reviews the entire file and makes a decision on whether to pay or deny the claim or compromise the claim in some way.

He usually will seek the guidance of an outside counsel before he makes the decision. The outside counsel is an attorney we hire who looks at the claim from an outside, independent viewpoint as to coverage and evidence that we have. They are trained in courtroom defense, examination under oaths, and depositions. We feel that is a safeguard from getting hit with a bad-faith verdict, and it has worked great for us.

I mean this sincerely and not as an insurance company ploy. We do give the insured every benefit of the doubt, and we are fair to insured's. If my company was not fair to every insured, I would not work for them.

There have been several times that I thought I had enough evidence to take a case to trial and have the company deny the claim, but either our attorney or the company would weigh everything and pay the claim over my objection, so to speak, because they didn't think there was enough to convict the insured. On the other hand, there have been times that I thought we did not have enough evidence to go to trial and the claim was denied.

The best thing about handling the claim this way is that anytime the claim is denied and I am in depositions prior to trail or actually on the stand in front of a jury in trial, if I am asked the question, "Why did you deny this claim?" my answer is that I didn't. Then they asked, "You were the investigator, right?" I answer, "Yes, but the home office supervisor denied the claim."

In many court cases I have been in, the insured's attorney has not done his homework, and then they ask me right in the middle of the trial, "Well, where is this supervisor?"

I answer, "In Cincinnati, Ohio."

We are in the middle of a court case, the jury is seated and impatient, and the attorney has blown his case because the person who denied the claim isn't in the courtroom. It is pretty hard to submit a bad-faith claim to the jury without the person testifying as to why the claim was denied.

Back to the Iranian case. It was my turn to give my deposition, and I had been waiting. I had prepared three days for this, reading every word in my file, every statement I had taken, and every source of evidence I had.

At one point I was asked how this fire occurred and who I thought set the fire.

I said, "I don't know if this is true or not, but...

(You have to remember that everything I say in a deposition is transcribed and put into the jury room for the jury to read, and in a large case they do read the depositions.)

"....I was told in my investigations that the insured is a fake Bible-thumping Christian. He makes his kids watch while he has sex with his girlfriend, he was the one who cut her when she was supposedly attacked, he was the one who faked the Barbie dolls and the blood on them to throw us off, and he is in debt to the tune of about $150,000. He cannot sell any of his paintings, and I have spoken with a real Civil War artist, and he says that on a scale of one to ten, the insured is about a two. He said his prints have not and will never sell to anyone. I then said that John had thousands of worthless prints that he was stuck with, he increased his coverage right before the fire, he took his Bible and gun out of the fire before he set it, and then he must have poured twenty gallons of gasoline on the fire and then set it, burning his building down." I then said that the thing that he really screwed up on was not faking a forced entry into the building. I told the attorney that I had the rear door lock and it was in the locked position. The insured had the only key. I told him that if he had faked the forced entry, he probably would have got away with burning his building down, but he really messed up.

I then just said, "That's what happened. Your client burned down his own building, and I can prove it. Let's go to trial."

The one thing you have to really admire about my company is the fact that in this case, John sued us for the claim and bad faith. In the state that this case occurred in, they had an unlimited amount that you could sue for the bad-faith accusation.

The insured sued us for the assets of the company. Think about this—the buildings, all of the chairs, cars, money, everything. My company is not small, and the assets are huge.

We went for it and were ready to put everything the company owned on the line to fight insurance fraud. I don't know how you would feel, but I was sweating bullets even though I knew John had set the fire and we would win, but there is always that doubt in the back of your mind as to what a jury will do. This was really scary.

I was at home on a Sunday night. The trial was set to begin on Monday morning, and I had to drive several hours to get to the courthouse. My stomach was in knots, and I was wondering at the end of the three-day trial whether or not I would even have a job.

My home phone rang, and it was our attorney. He said, "Don't bother to show up for trial tomorrow. We have settled the case." I was furious; I had not been consulted in any way. I had worked for about two years on this case, countless hours of investigation, driving, and sweat.

I asked our attorney who made this call. He said, "Calm down. It is really good news," and he told me of the settlement.

He said that after my deposition, the insured and his attorney got very concerned about things that would come out at trial, and they wondered if they would win or not.

I cannot tell you what the insured settled for, because that was one of the stipulations that I could not talk about the settlement. I can tell you that the attorney for the insured had accumulated several thousand dollars in his defense of the case. I know this was paid, but I know the insured did not buy anything that year with the rest. Enough said.

Sometimes we settle a case for ten cents on the dollar, sometimes five cents on the dollar, and sometimes less than that. I will let you wonder what we actually gave them to go away. Let's put it this way: I walked into work on Monday morning with a huge smile on my face, and this was probably the biggest dollar amount win that I have had in my career or probably ever will have.

I feel this case was a win and it was due to the diligence and through news of our attorney that worked this case. Drew, you are one of the best!

GETTING THIS OFF MY CHEST!

This next chapter is going to seem a little unbelievable. It is about a fraud claim that took me three years to finish, was the most devastating thing I have ever had to do, really got me down physically, mentally, and emotionally, and ruined two friendships that I had had for several years.

It ended with an attorney who was a friend of mine hating me and another attorney that was a good friend and a college professor of mine hating me so much that at his trial, his parents spit on my shoes as I walked by and cursed me in several different languages, including Hebrew.

This case went from a civil trial to a criminal trial and then back to a civil matter, and I will explain all of this in this chapter because I know that is confusing.

The claim was a burglary of the insured's law office. Let's call him Lloyd. Lloyd's claim was a $50,000 burglary of his law office. My company spent $80,000 defending this case. I want you to put yourself in my place for a moment.

Lloyd was your friend, and the claim was $50,000. Why not pay the claim, and you would have saved $30,000? You would probably say, just pay the claim!

The only answer that I have for that is you are right; I was wrong. I wish I had never seen this claim. I wish I had let someone else work it and the claim had been paid. I would still have my friend, who was the insured, and we would probably be better friends than we were because I would have closed my eyes when he did this and he would have been paid the money he needed.

The attorney who represented him would also still be my friend instead of hating me to this day and refusing to even acknowledge that I breathe the same air as he does.

I will not mention any names or cities, but everyone who knows me, including this attorney and Lloyd, will know what I am talking about, and you will know that this is what really happened.

I will first go back to when I was a highway patrolman. I was attending college, and one of my instructors in criminology was this attorney. We hit it off very well, and I respected him. He had been a police officer, working night shifts and attending law school during the day. He used to joke about his partner being the only thing that got him through law school. They rode together, and when they didn't have a call to go on, his partner would let him sleep so he could stay awake in class the next day. He eventually graduated and became an attorney. I didn't know at that time what a dark side being an attorney involved. In the insurance industry, any attorney that represents insured's for fraud cases is known as being on the dark side. We are the good guys, and they are the bad guys.

I knew that this attorney was on the dark side, and I had worked several cases with him, he being the insured's attorney and me being the SIU guy investigating the loss and many times denying the claim as a result of the investigation. We still got along, and if there was one thing I knew about this friend it was this: if you called his office, you were being recorded. He recorded every call that came into his office, without any exception. I want you to remember this fact, because this is what eventually broke this case wide open, and I used this personal knowledge against him to win the case.

If I had this to do over again, I would not have done it. Again, I hate losing friends, and I did in this case, big time.

Let's now talk about Lloyd. I met him through a mutual friend of mine. I can use his name because I know he won't mind, and he will probably like to see his name in print. Mike is my best friend. I broke him in as a pupil on the state patrol, he is a former marine, and we hit it off from the first day we met. We are still friends, but he has a bad heart, and I only wish that he lives long enough to see this book published. He is known as "mean Mike," and he is really nuts. There is nothing that he would not do and nothing I would put past him. He would do anything for me, and I would do anything for him, even die, and everyone who knows the two of us will tell you that. We both have the same beliefs and know that when we die, we will see each other in heaven, so it really doesn't matter which one of us goes first. I feel sorry for God if Mike goes first, because everyone else who goes after him will have to stand in line for years, because Mike has millions of questions to ask him.

The mutual friend of Mike's and mine turned out to be Lloyd. I got to know Lloyd personally over the years. I first met him at a gun show. All three of us love guns and gun shows.

We met for breakfast, and we hit it off really well. Over the next few years, I saw him at several gun shows and had lunch with him occasionally.

He was a dark-side attorney, but I liked him. He and the attorney that represented him in this burglary case (my college professor in criminology) were also good friends.

I would occasionally get calls from Lloyd, and he would have a questionable auto accident that he wanted me to look at. I was a really good accident reconstructionist due to investigating accidents for ten years and all of the training that I had at the highway patrol academy. I can tell how fast a car was going prior to impact in any accident, and this can be huge when it comes to liability and tort law, percentage of negligence, last clear chance to avoid, etc.

Lloyd would just ask some technical questions about a case that he was working on, and I would give him advice as long as my company was not involved in the case. He never paid me anything other than a lunch every now and then. I would then buy the next lunch we had together. I did this because we were friends.

I would go to an accident scene, tell him what I found, do some skid-mark analysis for him, let him know if his client was in the right or wrong, and then he would take it from there. It was understood that this was advice only and I would never testify to this in court. I also received valuable information from him as to the mindset of plaintiff, or bad-guy attorneys, as we call them.

I still remained friends with his attorney that would represent him later.

This went on for several years, and then the lunches, calls, and requests for help became less frequent, and then they just stopped.

I heard on the news that Lloyd had been found naked in his condo, under the influence of drugs, and he had been arrested for this as well as several gun charges for illegal guns that they found in his apartment when the police answered the 911 call.

As a result of this, the insured lost his license to practice law.

When the claim first came in, I got called into my boss's office. He said, "We have a new burglary claim on an attorney that I want you to handle. It has many red flags, and you may even know this guy."

He told me the name, and I told my boss that we used to be good friends but I had not heard from him in a while. I told my boss that I had heard on the news that he had been arrested and things were not going well for him. He said, "That is the biggest red flag. He is an attorney who has lost his license, and now we get a claim on him where his business office has been burglarized and everything in his office was stolen, and the claim is about fifty thousand dollars."

I told my boss that he should get someone else to handle this because I knew the insured and I would rather not get involved. He said, "If you know him and were friends, who would give him a better shake than you?"

I said, "Probably no one," and I agreed to handle the claim, not knowing at that time that what I had just gotten myself into would cost me dearly—the loss of two friends, many sleepless nights, and still watching over my back for a bullet that may come at any time. Even to this day, I regret listening to my boss and not giving this case to someone else.

I reviewed the file and saw many problems with the case. I thought, *if an attorney doesn't have a license to practice any longer, what does he not need any longer?* The answer came back again and again: his office. I have always kept an open mind on every claim I have worked until such time as the evidence leads me to believe that the insured is lying to me or has committed fraud based on the evidence I have gathered. My boss again has always said, "Your job is to gather facts, and that is it. Don't become personally involved in any case, keep an open mind, and above all, do not take any case personally, or it will ruin you." This one almost did because I did take it personally.

I did something in this case that I had never done before. I still don't know to this day if I did anything ethically wrong. It was not illegal in any way, nor did it constitute bad faith, but was I right? I don't know to this day.

I called Lloyd and started a general conversation with him, asked him how things were going, and then I told him I had been assigned to his burglary. He seemed glad about this.

I want to mention one thing about Lloyd.

He was a very devout Jew. I taught a Sunday school class (and still do) at a Methodist church and had about twenty kids that ranged from thirteen to eighteen, and I had my hands full. They had many questions about other religions, and I asked Lloyd one Sunday prior to his arrest to come to my church and explain to

my class all about the Jewish religion. I told him I would reciprocate with his students at his synagogue, but he never called me to.
He was very good and put my students on the spot, asking them
many questions about their faith that they could not answer, and
for many weeks I had to teach them how to answer questions
about the Christian faith if they were asked by the Jewish faith
about what they believe. He was very good and knew his faith.

He went on to tell me that he started using drugs after he
asked his girlfriend to marry him. He was devastated when she
said to him that he was a good boyfriend but he didn't have
enough money to ask her to marry him. This crushed Lloyd, and
he went downhill from there. He started using drugs and ended
up being found in a drug-induced stupor in his apartment, which
led to his arrest and him losing his license to practice law.

I told him I was very sorry for everything he had been through
and told him he should have stayed in touch. He responded that
I should have also, and this really put me in my place, like I had
failed him.

I would fail him again before this was all over.

I explained to Lloyd that I would have to investigate his claim
because that was what I did. I told him that since we were friends
there were a lot of questions on his claim, and if there was anything wrong that he should tell me now and I would let him
withdraw the claim and the entire matter would be closed.

When I told you before that I didn't know if this was ethical
or not, this was the reason. I have never done this to an insured
before I have started my investigation.

I did, however, feel that since Lloyd was a friend, I should give
him this one chance to just make the whole thing go away. I told
him again, "I have to investigate this. If there is anything wrong
with it in any way, please withdraw your claim."

He said that nothing was wrong, that his office had been broken into, and he had insurance and wanted to make the claim.

I said okay and that I needed to see his office and take a statement from him.

I met with him a few days later, took his statement, and the entire time I saw a side of him that I had never seen before; he was actually cocky with me and demeaning.

This offended me because I thought we were friends, and as my boss had told me, "You will give him the benefit of the doubt more than anyone."

I started having my doubts, because this was not the same person I had known before his arrest.

I told him to make a list of items that were stolen and to send them to me as soon as possible.

I received the list and started checking items out. Some items he said he owned and purchased did not pan out when I actually checked with the stores he said he purchased them from.

Even though some of the stores said that he did not purchase the items from them, I gave him the benefit of the doubt, and if nothing else was wrong with the claim, I would probably advise the company to pay it since I had no hard evidence that it was a fraud at this point.

That was when I received a call from the police officer that handled the investigation. I knew this officer from my career as a state trooper. He said that he doubted the theft occurred and he thought that the case stunk. I asked him if he had any evidence, and he said, "Just rumors at this point."

This was interesting in the fact that later on in the case when we were in trial, this same officer was called to testify, and he denied ever telling me this and actually said that I had called him and told him that I thought the insured was lying. I had never said this, and I was totally devastated that a police officer would lie like this on the stand in front of a jury. Can you spell "*pay off*?"

I then received a call from a deputy sheriff that I know, and he said, "I think you need to come to the jail and interview an inmate we have." I asked him why, and he said that the inmate had started talking about a burglary he committed and was trying to rat out a guy who hired him to fake a burglary at his office. He wanted to tell his story to someone so he could get his own charge reduced or dismissed by being an informant. They told him that they didn't know what he was talking about.

The informant, let's call him Jake, said the case had to do with the Cincinnati Insurance Company. The deputy knew me, and he called me to tell me this.

I dropped what I was doing, drove to the sheriff's department, and obtained permission to interview Jake with a tape recorder, which is a huge obstacle, but not if you know deputies and have worked with them for years.

I met with Jake and asked him why he was coming forward, and he said, "To get my sentence reduced." If an informant tells me up front why they are giving information and are honest about it, usually they are telling the truth. But I always try to verify what they have told me. In this case, he said that Lloyd was his attorney on a case several years ago and represented him in a burglary. He said he got a call from Lloyd, and Lloyd asked him to commit a burglary at his office because he needed the insurance money. Lloyd told him he could sell any of the items he took from the office, but he wanted him to commit the burglary as soon as possible because he needed the insurance money.

Lloyd had told him what was in the office, what he could take, what he couldn't take, exactly how to get in, and said the alarm would not be set.

When I had asked Lloyd about the alarm, which did not go off that night, he just said he had forgotten to set the alarm that night. Convenient?

I took a recorded statement from Jake, and he even told me where he had sold the items, to what fence, and what he got for each item. A fence is a person that a burglar goes to and takes his stolen items to for either money or drugs, usually drugs.

I reported the case to the home office and what I had in evidence. They stated that we would hire an attorney and have Lloyd submit to an examination under oath.

Before that happened, the sheriff's department stated that even though the local police had dropped the investigation, they still had jurisdiction in that area and they wanted to take the case to the prosecutor.

This really upset the original investigating officer who later would lie on the stand.

They sent me a letter requesting a copy of my file and a copy of the statement that the Jake had given to me. They did reduce the charge against the informant for his statement to me.

I was in the process of cooperating with the prosecutor on criminal charges against Lloyd for insurance fraud when I received the call that will haunt me forever, and what I did at that point broke this case wide open but at the same time, lost me a good friend. The call was from Lloyd's attorney.

I knew that this attorney taped all phone calls, which is legal in the state that it occurred in as long as the person taping the call is a party to the conversation. So as soon as he called me, I started my tape recorder.

I started the tape, and he said, "Jack, this is_____. How you doing? Long time no see, my friend." I answered that everything was going well and it was good to hear from him. He then said, "Jack, I have been hired by Lloyd to represent him in this case. We all know each other, and we are friends. I have heard some things and have spoken to Lloyd about the claim. We both know that many of the items he claimed, he exaggerated; well, most of the items he exaggerated, so why can't we just forget about those items and you pay him for the items that he really had stolen. We will send you a list of the real things stolen and the ones that he lied about—we will just forget about them, okay?"

I was in shock. I had never, ever had this happen to me before, and I had it on tape. I had an attorney lying for another attorney, trying to get him out of fraud charges, and probably the only reason he called me was they had heard about my informant.

I told the attorney that Lloyd needed to drop his claim now and this was the only way that this would go away. I told him that all Lloyd had to do was exaggerate one item and it voided the policy. He said he disagreed and they would still come after us for the claim.

I probably should have told the attorney about the pending charges at that time, but I could not. The sheriff was conducting an investigation that could lead to felony charges against Lloyd, and I could not interfere with that.

I just told the attorney that I could not do that and would have to continue my investigation. He became very upset with me, and the conversation ended.

I took the tape to the prosecutor, and she just smiled. I felt terrible. I had to do my job on this one, but I did not like what I had to do. I was caught in the middle, so to speak.

Charges were filed against Lloyd for insurance fraud, and his claim was denied by my company.

We could deny the claim due to the provision in the policy concerning falsification. Anytime anyone falsifies documents, alters documents, lies about items being taken, or misrepresents things that occurred, the policy is void back to the date that it was taken out. It is as if the policy never existed, and the premium that they paid is refunded to them.

In regards to the criminal charges, Lloyd committed insurance fraud when he lied about the items he had taken and attempted to get paid for them. The prosecutor had the tape of the insured's own attorney as evidence against Lloyd. What Lloyd's attorney didn't know was that we had the tape. He did not know when he tried to make this deal with me that I was recording his conversation; the same way that I knew he was recording me.

At this point in the claim investigation, I started to really have second thoughts.

I was in the process of putting the screws to two friends, and I was sick about it. I had tried to get them to back away from the claim, once to Lloyd and once to his attorney, and they would not listen. Now I was at the point of no return.

I felt like Judas, but I had to do my job. I discussed the entire situation with my wife. Who is my best sounding board? She said to me, "You didn't do anything wrong. He did, and you need to stay focused on that."

The trial date approached for the criminal charges. Lloyd had refused any depositions on our claim denial because of the criminal charges and would not give us one until after the trial, which is his right. This goes along with the law of self-incrimination.

The trial was one of the worst things I have ever had to go through. I had two friends in the courtroom—well, two former friends—staring daggers through me the entire time I was there. Then it came time to call me to the stand. I had met with the prosecutor twice to go over the case. She said not to use the tape unless she gave me the go-ahead by nodding to me. She said that Lloyd's attorney had to open the door for us to be able to use the tape. I agreed.

I was called to the stand, and they tried to put the notion in front of the jury that I was not a friend of Lloyd's, had never gone to gun shows with him, had never eaten with him, etc. This was to totally discredit my entire testimony and make it look like I was just out to get Lloyd on these charges.

At one point the attorney was badgering me pretty good on the stand, and then he said to me, "Mr. Morgan, why or what made you start this investigation against my client that led us eventually here to this courtroom today?" And he turned and smiled smugly to the jury. I answered him with two words: "You did!"

He looked at me very funny, and started to follow up his question. Then he thought about it and walked back to his table.

I wondered," *Will he let this drop? Does he know I have the tape? What is he going to do?*

I was looking at the prosecutor, and she was sitting on the edge of her seat. She shook her head no and put her finger to her mouth, which meant, "Don't say a word!"

(As a side note, this prosecutor went on after this trial to become an outstanding judge.)

About two minutes went by, and he asked me several other questions about the case, but none about my comment.

He finally could not stand it any longer, and then he came back to the stand and very snotty, very cocky, very demeaning, said to me, "Mr. Morgan, you earlier were asked the question about why you started the investigation, and you said it was because of me. What did you mean by that?" He had just blown it, and he had no idea what was coming. I really didn't either. I had not thought about all of the implications what I had to say would make and the effects it would have on the trial. The prosecutor did, and she did not like this attorney at all. She wanted a piece of him, and I didn't even know it.

I looked at the prosecutor; she nodded her head, smiled at me, and mouthed the word, *now.*

I then answered, "Mr. Attorney, about six months ago, when your client, Lloyd, presented his claim to my company, I asked him to withdraw his claim, and he refused. Then you called me, told me that Lloyd had committed fraud, and asked if we could just ignore the items that were exaggerated and go ahead and pay him for some of the items? I told you I could not do that."

With my statement out there, the courtroom went crazy, the judge went crazy, and the attorney went crazy. Lloyd was standing hollering at me, "Liar, liar." His family was standing and shouting at me. Everyone in the courtroom was out of control except for me and the prosecutor; she just sat there smiling and waiting. So I did also.

The judge cleared the courtroom except for me, the prosecutor, the court recorder, the bailiff, the attorney, and his client, Lloyd.

The judge leaned over to me and said, "Mr. Morgan. You have just made a very strong accusation that could turn this entire trial around. It could cause the accused to be found guilty and sentenced, it could cause sanctions against his attorney, or it could put you in jail for lying on the stand. I surely hope that you can prove what you just said."

I again looked at the attorney, and she nodded again and smiled. I took the tape out of my pocket and said, "Yes, I can prove it, Judge," and handed him the tape. I said, "This is the phone conversation with the Lloyd's attorney."

Lloyd's attorney gasped, started yelling and hollering, and said that the tape was not admissible and that the judge needed to chastise me for embarrassing him in the courtroom and lying.

The judge looked at the prosecutor, and she simply stood up and said, "Judge, it is a well-known fact that Lloyd's attorney tapes all of his phone calls, and Mr. Morgan was just protecting himself against something that may happen further down the road in his investigation, and this is one of those times."

The judge stated that in this state, as long as one party is in the conversation, they can legally tape the voice of the other party. He said, "Mr. Morgan, are you the other party?" I said, "Yes, You're Honor, and that tape has not been out of my possession at any time since I taped it, and I have not altered it in any way."

The judge said the court would be in recess while he reviewed the tape.

He came back out and called everyone back into the courtroom.

He said that the statement I had made concerning what happened with the phone call to Lloyd's attorney would stand and he had reviewed the audio tape.

He then called Lloyd to the front of the courtroom and asked him if he wished to continue with the trial with this attorney or seek another attorney and ask for a continuance until he could hire one.

Lloyd shocked everyone when he said he wanted to stay with the same attorney.

I knew then that Lloyd had just made the biggest mistake in his life. He should have asked for a mistrial and started another one. He didn't.

I knew right then that we had won the case.

Lloyd's attorney declined to ask me any other questions, and I was excused from the witness stand. The prosecution rested, and the defense tried to show what a great guy Lloyd was and that all of these accusations were a mistake. He even went further to say that the only reason his client was here today was the fact that the sheriff's department had it in for him because he represented criminal clients and had repeatedly made them look bad.

They finally rested, and the prosecutor just sat there with a grin on her face.

The jury was given their instructions, and I thought everything spoken by the judge was correct and to the point.

The jury came back in three hours and found Lloyd guilty of insurance fraud, and he was sentenced to six years in jail.

The family was devastated, Lloyd was shocked, and his attorney was shocked.

I was shocked and could not believe that he got the max, so to speak. I don't think the judge liked what his attorney had tried to do to me on the phone, but I might be wrong. Maybe he just didn't like Lloyd or his attorney, I don't know.

The prosecutor thanked me for my assistance, but I was not in a thankful mood. Lloyd was escorted from the courtroom in handcuffs and taken directly to jail. His relatives and family formed a gauntlet outside of the courtroom, and when I left they spit at my feet and cursed me. Lloyd's attorney passed me and said, "I hope you are proud of yourself."

I was not. I felt terrible, and this was not a time where I felt like I had done my job for my company. I knew that someone had to investigate the claim, but I kept thinking, *why did you take this on? Why didn't you refuse?* "You would give Lloyd the benefit of the doubt" kept coming back and haunting me. I had really blown it and put a man in jail and lost two friends at the same time and had spit all over my shoes and suit pants.

About six months went by, and I got a very upsetting call from the prosecutor. She said that she had bad news for me—Lloyd, acting as his own attorney, had appealed his case. The appeals court had reviewed the judge's instructions to the jury, found him at fault in some of the instructions, and had upheld the plea for a new trial and dismissed the original guilty finding of the jury. The prosecutor said this was not the only bad news. The county prosecutor, her boss, had decided that he would not retry the case and Lloyd would go free. The county did not have the funds or the time to start another trial.

I argued with her that this just set my company up for a lawsuit of all lawsuits, and she said she was sorry but there was nothing she could do.

I heard Lloyd was released the next day.

Then the worst happened. About one week after Lloyd got out of jail, a deputy showed up at the office with a lawsuit that Lloyd had filed against me personally and my company. He had filed suit against the company for many millions of dollars, but I cannot remember how much. I do remember the figure against me. He filed suit against me personally for malicious prosecution for $350 million.

My company immediately hired an attorney to represent them, and then they hired the best defense attorney in my state to represent me on this case.

To not bore you with the details that lasted over the next year, there were hearings and depositions where I had to sit across the table from Lloyd and listen to him try to bash me and try to get me to say that everything I said was a lie.

Lloyd would get his case together and file it, we would file our answer and ask for a summary judgment, and we would win. We did this three times over the next year, winning every decision by the courts for our summary judgment, which means Lloyd loses everything.

He finally appealed the case before the Ohio Supreme Court, and when we got the decision back that they had voted in our favor, it was a great day for me.

I still feel bad for Lloyd. I had tried to get him to withdraw the case from the start, and he wouldn't listen to me. But justice had been done, and the case was finally over.

THIS FAMILY
WAS NOT THE
CLEAVERS

To start this chapter, when I was a child there was a show on TV called *Leave It to Beaver*. It was a show about a very wholesome family that lived by values and good old' American pie ideals. Their last name was Cleaver.

This chapter is not about a family that resembled the Cleavers in any way.

This case is probably the most unusual in the fact that it had everything in it—fire, arson, attempted murder, child endangerment, cross dressing, lesbian lovers, 400-pound women, a 150-pound man, tales of unbelievable police reports, lying, twenty years in jail, and child homosexuality taught by a father to son. Wow, how do I get all of that into one chapter?

Any of the above topics in itself is not really a big deal. I have been a cop and have seen just about everything there is to see, except all of this in one family was a little hard to take. When compared to the old TV show *Leave It to Beaver*, this family, as the chapter reflects, was not the Cleavers.

I am not saying there is anything wrong with homosexuality or any of the things I will speak about. I am not bashing heavy women or thin men. I am just telling the story as it is. Let's start at the beginning. I, as usual, received a call from an adjuster— I will call him Fitz: "I have a really weird one on my hands." He said that he had an insured with a wife and son who had a kitchen fire. He moved them out of their home while the smoke and fire damage was being repaired. They were staying in a hotel until their house was ready to move back into. He said a weird thing happened that day. He said that they were cleaning up the smoke and fire damage from the first fire and they discovered that someone had entered the house and tried to blow it up.

The wife, Jackie, came home to check on the repairs when she got off of work the night before and smelled gas, so she called the fire department, and they found that a hole had been drilled in the main gas line from the main source to the water heater. The fire chief said that she was really lucky she had smelled the gas and called the fire department.

I drove to the house and met with the fire department arson investigator. I also hired a cause-and-origin investigator to check out the scene and collect any evidence.

My first thought was that vandals had broken into the house and tried to cause the house to explode. There were no accelerants poured or any accelerant used anywhere in the house.

When I got to the scene, I checked the gas line and discovered that the hole had been drilled. I worked with the cause-and-origin expert and discovered that a 3/4-inch bit had been used the drill through the line.

The fire department said that the smell of gas was so strong that they had to use fans to get it out of the house, and they did an emergency evacuation of houses that were within two hundred yards of the house itself. They said that if a spark had occurred, it would have blown the insured's home to bits, and probably two houses on either side of the insured's home would have gone with it.

The first thing I did was check for any forcible entry, and there was none. Then the cause-and-origin expert called me over and said, "What door did the insured's wife come in when she entered the house?" I called Jackie and asked her, and she said the kitchen door. I also asked her why she had come to the house that night so late. It happened about a quarter after midnight. She said that she came in through the kitchen door to check out the carpet that had been laid that day. She worked in a video store, and her husband, Bill, had called her about nine o'clock that evening and told her she needed to go by the house when she got off work to check out the carpet that had been laid that day. The cause-and-origin expert said that the weird thing was that the light switch that was by the kitchen door was not connected. I called the contractor who was working on the house, and he said, "I thought that we had done that; I guess we didn't. We will take care of that tomorrow." I told him that by him not connecting the switch, he had probably saved Jackie's life.

The cause-and-origin expert said that in a small house like this was, if the gas had built up for several hours, as the fire department thought by the strong smell, if the switch had been connected and the wife had flipped it, it was very possible that would have been enough to ignite the gas and cause an immediate and highly dangerous explosion, probably destroying the entire house.

I had the fire department disconnect the pipe that had been drilled, and I hired a plumber to come out and fix the damage and make sure the house was safe at this point.

I then interviewed Jackie at her hotel. Jackie was a large woman, weighing approximately four hundred pounds, with short brown hair, who dressed in a very matronly fashion, and my first impression was that she was a dominated woman, possibly abused physically or mentally. I asked her to start at the beginning when they had the initial kitchen fire. She said that on the day of the fire, she thought it was unusual that Bill had asked to cook the evening meal. He was frying chicken on the stove in an iron skillet. He then asked her to go and get gas with him while they left their son, Scott, at the house. Jackie said she asked Bill if he turned off the skillet, and Bill said yes, and he was insistent that she go with him to get gasoline in his car, which he had never done before. She didn't know why, but she went with him.

On their way back home, the fire department was seen at their home and they were putting out a kitchen fire. Scott had barely escaped and gotten out before he was injured. The fire damaged several rooms in the homes, but the house was not a total loss. The fire department got there very quickly and put the fire out. Scott had discovered the fire and ran to neighbors, who called the police.

A week later, after the family had been moved to a hotel while the repairs were being conducted, Jackie said that Bill had called her at work from the house about nine o'clock and told her to go by the house at midnight when she got off of work to check out the carpet that was installed earlier that day. Jackie didn't think anything about it and did what he asked. When Jackie got to the house, she unlocked the kitchen door and opened it. She felt for the light switch and flipped it, but no light came on. Jackie was just about to go to another switch when she smelled the strong gas odor and knew that something was wrong. Jackie immediately went next door to a neighbor and called the fire department. When fire officials arrived, they conducted an investigation and told Jackie about the hole that had been drilled into the main gas line.

I asked Jackie where her husband was at the time of the fire, and she said that he was at the hotel with her son.

I inquired if Jackie was having any marital problems. She said things were just fine between her and Bill, but instantly I knew she was lying to me. I had developed a baseline on Jackie at the start of the interview. When she recalled information that I knew to be truthful stored information, she looked up and to the left; but when I asked her about the marital problems, she looked up and to the right, which meant she was going to the opposite side of the brain for edited or fabricated information.

Jackie also rubbed her nose, and her eye blink rate increased dramatically. At this point I knew she was lying to me.

"Jackie, are you telling me the truth?" I asked empathetically.

She hesitantly said that she had not been truthful with me and that she and Bill were having problems but hoped they could get things worked out.

I asked where her husband was at the moment, and she said Bill was at work. I called him on his cell phone and asked him if I could meet with him. He agreed. Bill worked about twenty minutes away at an apartment complex, where he was the maintenance man.

I know some of you are thinking, *Maintenance man, drill, 3/4-inch bit?* Okay, I did also, but remember the insured always is given the full benefit of the doubt, and I keep an open mind with every claim that I work.

I drove to where he was working and interviewed him in one of the apartments he was working on.

The first thing I saw when I met with Bill, a slight man—maybe 150 pounds soaking wet—was that he had a toolbox open with several screwdrivers out and he was working on cabinets. I also noticed a drill in his toolbox. There was no bit in it, and I didn't see any bits lying around. I wondered if he might have another toolbox in his truck.

I mentioned his weight for one reason and that is that Bill's weight has significance later in this story.

I started the interview, and within fifteen minutes, I knew he was lying to me. There is a deception tool in interviewing called gaze aversion. It is when someone cannot look you in the eye from the time you get there until you leave; this is total deception.

From the time I met Bill, shook his hand, took a one-hour recorded interview, and left, he never looked at me in the eye...never!

This is a total, 100 percent red flag that I use all of the time.

I asked Bill about the kitchen fire, and he said he had no idea why he had asked his wife to go to the gas station with him.

He stood there looking down at the kitchen table near the cabinets he was working on and stared at it for one hour, sometimes drawing a circle with his finger on the countertop.

I asked him why he had called his wife, and he really didn't have a reason for that either. I asked him how long he had been at the house. He said he was there at nine o'clock, when he called Jackie. I asked him if he saw anything wrong at that time, and he said no. He had no idea who would have tried to blow his house up, and he had no enemies.

Usually when someone is innocent of fraud, they will do everything they can to help me. They will give me people who might have it out for them or give me some reason as to why someone would do this, and he had none. He was not going to cooperate in any way.

I asked Bill if he had drilled the gas line, and he said, "Why would I do something like that?" The old proverbial question with a question, which equals total deception.

I didn't have the evidence yet, but something was wrong here. Bill was exhibiting clear signs of avoidance. He had lied to me about his involvement with the gas line.

I decided not to pursue the questioning any further at that time. Any additional questioning needed to be done by the police, as I knew at this point a search warrant was needed for Bill's truck, an option only available to law enforcement.

I had a hunch that the drill bit in question was there in the toolbox in Bill's truck. The shavings I thought would still possibly be on the drill bit, and we could hopefully match them up to the material from the brass pipe in the house.

I ended the interview with Bill, but not before asking him the punishment question, which I always ask of an insured that has a fire, burglary, or theft. I asked Bill, "What do you think should be done to the person who did this?"

A typical response from an innocent person is, "Take them out to the first tree and hang them. They almost killed my wife!" I am sure you get the picture of what someone should say, when someone who has experienced trauma like this inflicted upon them. They feel violated.

Bill's answer was, "Maybe they had a reason to do this?" Not quite the answer you would expect from an innocent man.

I nearly screamed when he said this. The scale had just tipped against him, all the way to the floor. I had not completed my investigation, but I would have bet my next paycheck that I was right on this one: Bill had done this himself, and he had meant to kill his wife. I left hurriedly, almost in a panic. I kept thinking; *I am not dealing with a simple gas line leak, but an attempted homicide!*

I drove directly to the police department that had jurisdiction over this case. I simply walked in, asked for the detective section, and when I went in I said, "Have any of you guys ever had the SCAN class or studied the Reid Technique?" One detective raised his hand and said, "Mr. Morgan, how you doing? What can I do for you?"

When I heard my name, my jaw hit the floor. It was a young detective; let's call him John, who had played football with my son in high school. I had been the strength coach for the team, and he remembered me.

I again asked John about the two techniques after we had reminisced for a while.

John said he had been through both SCAN and Reid Technique classes and asked how he could help me.

I told John what happened on the case thus far—an intentionally-drilled hole in a gas pipe and my observations of gaze aversion, question-with-a-question, and the answer I got from Bill to the punishment question. (That's a cluster if I've ever seen one; three strikes and you're out!)

John replied simply, "You have got to be kidding me."

I said no, and then I told John that I would work with him on the case but that it was important that our investigations be kept separate. I told him about the interview, the drill, there not being any bits visible, and the possibility of the bit being in the insured's truck.

John said that he wanted me to wait where I was while he called the prosecutor. John returned, saying that they should have a search warrant, based on what I had told him, within one hour.

The warrant was issued for a search of Bill's truck.

I went to the apartment building where Bill worked with the detectives. I stayed in the car and waited. They went inside and first did an interview, and then they came outside, accompanied by a very worried-looking Bill.

I have seen this look before, and I saw it plain as day on Bill now—the head raised to the sky, the long sigh, and the chin against his chest; the signs of an imminent confession.

They opened up his truck, and I just stood there watching. Bill gave me some very hard looks as the police started the search on his truck but didn't say anything to me.

The detectives found another tool bag in the truck. They went through it and found a 3/4-inch drill bit that had brass metal shavings on it. The police officers conducting the search advised Bill that the game was over. They said they had brought the section of drilled brass pipe from Bill's home, along with the shavings from underneath it. In comparing the shavings on the drill bit to the gas line pipe and the shavings from his home, the police told Bill that they were convinced they had found a match.

This is the biggest difference between law enforcement and the insurance industry as far as investigations goes. We cannot lie to any insured. This would be bad faith, and remember what that equals—usually about a million dollars. The police, meanwhile, had just lied to Bill. They didn't even have the pipe with them. But all it took was for them to tell Bill that they had the hard evidence against him and that they knew he did it. Bill looked skyward again. He again let out a sigh, and again his chin went to his chest. And sure enough, out came Bill's confession.

The police returned to searching Bill's truck. There was another bag inside. When the police opened it up, the bag was full of women's clothing. They checked the size, and the clothing would fit a woman about 150 pounds. The police knew that they were not his wife's, because there was no way these clothes could have fit her. They questioned Bill about the clothes, and he admitted that he was a cross dresser and they were his. Okay, this is when it started getting really weird.

Bill was asked if he wanted to give a statement without an attorney present, along with his confession. He said he did. This is his story.

Bill admitted to trying to kill his wife, Jackie. Bill said he had a girlfriend and they wanted to live together for the rest of their lives but his family was in the way. First, Bill had tried to kill his son, Scott, with the fire he set in the kitchen. When this didn't work, Bill saw an opportunity to murder his wife when the house was being repaired due to the kitchen fire so that Jackie's death might look like an accident resulting from the repair work. Bill went to the house at nine o'clock that night and drilled the hole in the pipe. He said that he first shut off the gas at the main and then drilled the hole in the pipe, after which he turned the gas back on. Bill said he was afraid of a spark if he drilled while the gas was on.

Bill confessed that he figured that three hours of the house filling with gas would be enough to blow up the kitchen with Jackie in it when she turned on the light switch. Bill admitted he didn't know that the contractor had not connected the power to the switch.

Bill never did tell us what his next plan to take his son Scott out of the picture was. Bill said that after his wife was dead, he was going "to ride off into the sunset" with his new girlfriend (who we found out later, as it so happens, was a woman larger than Jackie; the petite women's clothes in the truck were definitely Bill's.)

It gets better, folks.

Bill was charged with attempted murder, and he was going to enter a guilty plea. His wife, Jackie, had to be in court for the plea and the sentencing. I had been in contact with Jackie several times since Bill was arrested because of the insurance claim. There had been no additional damage from Bill drilling the hole in the gas main, but I could not actually prove that the first fire was intentional, so my company was running a separate standard investigation for a claim Jackie had filed for smoke damage done to items in the house as a result of the fire. Since I was so involved in this case and familiar with the claim, I conducted this investigation myself. I found that Jackie had submitted a fraudulent receipt for a large-screen TV that supposedly burned up in the fire. I discovered that the TV was worth about $500 and she tried to zap us for $2,500 using a fake receipt she had created and submitted; I just couldn't get away from this family.

I ran this by the company and asked what they wanted to do. My company was leery about denying Jackie's claim after what she had been through, and they didn't think a jury would think very highly of us for denying the claim because of an attempted fraud.

I just met with her at her home, and I was there to inform her that we were going to let the fraud slide, but she would only get $500 for the TV. When I went to the door, a black woman met me. I thought this was a little unusual, because the insured's wife is white.

When I introduced myself, Jackie came around the corner and told the black woman to let me in. She then embraced the black woman, and they kissed right there in front of me in the foyer. I really didn't know what to say, and I must have had a very surprised look on my face, because Jackie felt that it was her obligation to let me know that she was really a lesbian and had been faking it being married to a man, and now that her husband was locked up for a long while, she decided to live her life like it should be, with another woman.

They appeared together arm in arm at the trial, and Bill received twelve years in jail for the attempted murder.

About three weeks after Bill started his sentence, I got a call from John, the police detective I had worked with. He said, "Jack, you are not going to believe the news about our Cleaver family." He said that they got a call from the school principal about Bill's son, Scott. John said that Scott had been teaching other boys in his fifth and sixth grade classes how to give each other oral sex. When he was confronted about this and the police interviewed him, he admitted that his father had been the one to teach him how to do this.

When I started this story, I told you that the insured's were not the Cleavers; I only hope that anyone reading this will now agree with me.

I can only hope that I never, ever have another one that was as weird as this claim to investigate. One in my lifetime is way too much.

FIVE SHORT STORIES

The next five stories are about some really cool claims that I worked and busted, but they are really not long enough in the information to give a full chapter to each one. On each of the following investigations, I will tell you what was involved and the techniques I used to solve them. Some were from experience, and others were just plain old' luck.

THE JUDGE'S DAUGHTER

This claim involves a burglary that occurred while the insured was away from her condo for two days. She was a judge's daughter, and her name was Jill. The eventual handling and final decision of this claim took a lot of guts by the home office supervisor. We were lucky that Jill walked away from this claim.

The most interesting thing about this claim was that I could never come up with a motive for what she did. Jill had planned this theft for over one year; it had taken her that long to collect all of the receipts that she presented to us for payment. It would have taken a large moving truck to have emptied her home of the items she claimed. The total claim was about $150,000.

The legwork on this one was so intense that I called in the assistance of another investigator, Anthony (Ant-ney).

We were presented with a huge stack of receipts to prove that Jill owned all of the items she was claiming. You must realize that he burglars took "everything" in her home.

We each took half of the invoices, set up a room in a hotel to act as the base of operations, and started a huge spread sheet on the walls of the hotel, using flip-chart paper and taping up our findings.

We went to every business and department store where the receipts indicated a purchase was made. We listed each one on our sheets and then put the result of our personal contact with each store on the sheet also.

Jill had made the mistake of signing a form we call "the authorization to investigate the claim." This allows us to get anything we need for the investigation from any store. We had to make multiple copies of the form because most stores will not even speak to you without the form signed by the insured. This protects them if the insured would claim that they violated their privacy issues according to federal law.

Of the stacks of receipts that Jill submitted, here is the investigation results of a few of the items claimed. The first store I went to was Best Buy. Jill had stated she had purchased a video recorder from this store and that she had the credit card receipt for it. The total amount of the purchase was $1,200. I used the receipt because it had the serial number of the item on it. After speaking with the store manager and checking the store's records, we discovered that the video recorder had been purchased one day and then brought back the next. I then asked if they still had the video recorder. We went to their back room, and the recorder was on the shelf. I photographed the video recorder and put it and the original box on their copy machine. I made a copy of the serial number and model number and obtained a recorded statement from the store manager as to what had transpired. A copy of the charge slip where the amount of the video camera had been charged back to the insured's card was also obtained.

The second item was a $3,000 lamp from an antique store. I contacted the store where Jill had purchased the lamp. The store owner was cooperative and didn't even ask for a signed release. The invoice stated the lamp had been purchased for $3,000, had the date, and that it was paid for by check. The lamp was back in the store, and the owner described that the insured had purchased the lamp, obtained a receipt, then brought it back, asking them to tear up the check. The store invoice had "returned" on their copy, showed that the transaction had been cancelled, and the check had been voided.

Another item was an Oriental rug that was purchased out of California by mail. The receipt we had showed that the rug had been purchased for $10,000. I contacted the rug business in California and asked them to send me a copy of their original invoice. I never tell them what my copy says. I have found that sometimes the business is in collusion with the insured. The company asked me to fax them a copy of the authorization, and I did. They faxed me back the original invoice, which showed that the rug was sold for $1,000, not $10,000. The insured had whited out the original price and added a zero to the cost. This in itself is insurance fraud, and Jill could have gone to jail for seven years on this item alone.

I could go on and on and on. Every store or business we went to revealed the same result. Every item that had been purchased over the last year had been returned.

On the third day, our wall chart showed that every single receipt we had—and there were hundreds—was fraudulent. Each one had been changed or altered, the item taken back to the store, and the original receipt given to us. Jill had kept or destroyed all of the returned receipts.

I thought it was very interesting that at the end of the third day we received a call from an attorney. The attorney said that he was now representing Jill on her claim, and he was revoking our authorization and any evidence that we had found. I informed

Jill's new attorney that we would comply with his demand because that was the insured's right to do so, but anything we had collected up to the time of his call would still be used and was part of our file.

I told the attorney I would call him back after we completed our investigation and I would want to set up an appointment with him and Jill for an additional statement. He became very angry, said that "we could not do this," and that he would file a suit. I advised the attorney that if he did not cooperate with the investigation, that Jill's claim could be denied. He hung up on me.

Anthony and I compiled all of our information and drove to the local police department that had venue over the case. We did not have the luxury of contacting the State Insurance Commissioner's office Fraud Division. In the state that we were working, they didn't have division that did any enforcement of fraud claims. In most states when we discover a fraud claim, we have to report it to either the police or the fraud commission.

When we met with the police, it was as though we had just given them a Christmas present. The case was given to them wrapped in a tight bundle with nothing for them to do except meet with the prosecutor and have Jill arrested for fraud.

This arrest was not going to happen today. When the police saw what we had, they were excited about the locked-tight case until we told them who the insured was. When they discovered Jill was a judge's daughter, their whole attitude changed. The police said, "We are very sorry. Thanks for bringing this to us, but we would not touch this with a ten-foot pole." I was shocked, but that's politics.

This is where I played a game of insurance poker with Jill's attorney. Knowing that he would probably hear very soon that the police had no interest in the case, I knew I didn't have much time.

I called Jill's attorney and laid it on the line for him. I said, "Your client has filed a claim with us for $150,000. We have evidence in our file that every item she claimed was either returned to the store, the receipt was changed or altered to show a higher amount, or the checks or credit card charges were reversed. We have all of this evidence locked down tight." I then very calmly asked the attorney, "Does your client wish to proceed with this claim, or do you want to withdraw at this time?"

He said he would call me right back. I knew at that moment that the claim was over. Normally if an attorney has anything at all, he will wave his saber in the air, start accusations of slander, bad faith, we will sue you, etc. This never came out of his mouth. He said, "Let me check with my client, and I will call you back." I told Anthony when I hung up the phone that we would receive a call from the insured's attorney within ten minutes, and we made a bet. It was for dinner. In eight minutes, the phone rang, and it was the attorney. He said, "My client has done nothing wrong, and we resent your implications against her, but we have decided that we do not want to go through a long, drawn-out court case over this. We wish to withdraw our claim at this time," and he hung up.

I gave Anthony a high-five, and we prepared a report to the home office. We also sent the insured's attorney a letter stating that he had voluntarily given up his claim and no claim would be paid in any way to his client. I also sent him a voluntary cancellation of policy request and said that Jill needed to sign this form, because we didn't want to insure her any longer. I thought this may be pushing it a little bit, but I thought *what the heck? Let's give it a try.*

The next day I received a letter from Jill's attorney withdrawing the claim, stating that they would sign the cancellation of policy. This was just too sweet. We didn't pay a dime on the claim, and now we would be able to cancel the insured within forty-eight hours after the form was signed and we would be rid of her.

We had heard that the judge was really upset and that we dare not take a case in front of him, but luckily we never had to in his jurisdiction.

There were many times while handling this claim that I thought my days were numbered and had a strange feeling I was being followed, but I am still here, working to fight fraud. In this case, the checking of receipts saved my company $150,000.

Was justice served? No, but at least Jill didn't receive any money from the attempted fraud claim. If this would have been anyone other than a judge's daughter, she would have gone to jail for at least seven years. On this case, the wheel of justice had a crack in the spoke.

KUWAIT, HERE I COME!

I really love this case and the outcome of it. I took a chance at something I had never done before, and it paid off big time. The amount of this claim was not that large, only $10,000, but the outcome was something to go down in the fraud books as one of the funniest.

We insure tenant policies, which is where someone rents a house or apartment and takes out coverage on their contents. We usually insure these from ten to fifty thousand dollars.

I received the new claim from the adjuster, and he said the red flags were waving. The insured, let's call him Brian, was from Kuwait and had just turned in a loss for a $10,000 scheduled Rolex watch. A scheduled item is an item you pay an additional amount for to insure for any type of loss.

Brian had just taken out the policy thirty days before the theft. He said in the initial statement to the adjuster that he was in an airport and had his briefcase between his legs waiting on a plane. Brian said he fell asleep; someone stole the briefcase, and inside was the $10,000 Rolex watch. Brian had the receipt from the Assam Jewelry Exchange in Kuwait, and he gave it to our adjuster. The receipt said the watch was a fourteen-karat-gold Rolex and the price was $10,000.00. Being the sharp investigator I am I immediately saw a problem with the description. Can you tell what it was?

In many countries, especially Kuwait, the karat value is minimum eighteen karats, so I knew there was something questionable. The first thing I did was review the statement that the adjuster took, in which Brian stated that he had flown TWA the day the theft had occurred. I called TWA security and asked if anyone had filed a theft report that day for a Rolex watch. Security stated that Brian had filed a claim against the airport and TWA for the missing watch and had threatened to sue them if the watch was not paid for immediately.

Okay, now we have two problems, because you cannot file a claim for the same thing with two different entities. Brian had filed a claim with both TWA and my insurance company, which is illegal. I had them fax me a copy of the report, and he had used the same receipt with both TWA and our company. I ran a database check on Brian, and I could not find that he had ever existed anywhere. I could not find any criminal history on Brian or any prior claims, so I figured this was a first-timer and he really didn't know what he was doing. I did something on a whim that busted this case wide open. The receipt that he presented on our claim for the Rolex had an invoice number and a date. I picked up the phone and asked the operator if she could connect me long distance to Kuwait. She said no problem. I thought *this is going to be too easy.* I then got an operator in Kuwait and asked for any insurance company's name in Kuwait. She said, "That is easy. There is only one. The Kuwait Insurance Company." I had her connect me, and an adjuster answered the phone. I said, "You don't know me, but I am with a special investigations unit in the States, and I need a favor." The person on the other end said, "What do you need?" I told him that if he did me a favor, if he ever needed anything in the States, I would be glad to reciprocate for him. He agreed. I asked him if he knew of the Assam Jewelry Exchange. He said it was about two blocks from his office. I asked him to go to the exchange and see if they would give him a copy of the invoice number that Brian had given to me. The adjuster said it was no problem and he would fax it to me. The fax came in to my office the next day, and the invoice numbers matched, but there was one big problem. The invoice was in someone else's name, not Brian's, and the invoice was for a gold eighteen-karat necklace for $200.

I called Brian and asked him to meet with me at our law firm in Chicago. He agreed. I flew to Chicago and went to the address that Brian had listed on his policy before the meeting, just to check it out. The address was there, but it was a parking lot that had been abandoned, and there were no houses there at all. I then drove to the Chicago police department and met with a detective. The detective agreed to be there when Brian showed up and that he would be arrested for insurance fraud. I don't know what happened that day. Maybe the insured got cold feet or he got lost or whatever, but he did not show up, and when I called him, he would not answer his phone.

We sent him a letter denying his claim for non-cooperation, and we never heard from him again. The police did call me, and they were laughing. They said, "We just got a hit on Brian. He got tipped off somehow about our meeting and knew he was going to be arrested." He got on a plane and flew back to Kuwait. The ironic thing about this was the day he decided to fly back to Kuwait was three days before Kuwait was invaded by Saddam Hussein's troops. I wonder how things went for him there when that happened.

I called TWA and told them to forget about the claim Brian had filed with them. They just said thanks and hung up. The least they could have done was give me a free plane ticket, don't you think?

THE BIBLE SALESLADY

This case is also one of my favorites, because I used several techniques that I teach to bust this claim of this lady, if you could call her that. The end result of this claim investigation was the insured being found guilty of insurance fraud, and she was sentenced to five years in jail.

Her name is Mary. She was a Bible salesman, or salesperson. Excuse me...

Mary filed a claim against a large food store that we insure nationwide. Mary stated that she was just walking through the store and slipped on some baby oil when she fell, broke her hip, and possibly fractured her knee.

The first thing I did was run a database check on Mary, and it revealed that she had four other claims with stores where she had allegedly fallen down. In all of the claims, Mary alleged that there was baby oil on the floor, causing her falls. Mary had presented medical bills, had an attorney, and had been paid for all four claims in the amount of about $200,000.

I first thought, *Is this just coincidence, or does everyone have four falls in stores where they slipped on baby oil?* I thought that this actually happening to her would equate to standing on a hill every day in the same place and getting struck by lightning when the sun was out. I checked with the other companies that had similar claims with Mary, but they were very slow to react to my requests for their files. This is not unusual, because most companies are so afraid of getting hit with a suit for releasing personal information that they will not even talk to you.

The second thing I did was actually go to the store we insured and check with their security. Security did actually have a videotape of Mary falling. The video was in what we call multiplex, which is seven or eight cameras all going at the same time. To view multiplex easily, you have to go to a lab that can separate the tapes down into one camera and get a frame-to-frame copy. My company has our own forensic lab that can do this. I copied their tape, brought it back to our lab, and Mike, our forensic lab technician, made me a viewable copy. I saw on the tape that Mary had entered the store and had a cart. She walked around the store for about twenty-five minutes yet had put nothing into her cart. She just kept going down the same aisle several times for no reason.

As Mary approached a store display, I could see a shadowed figure in the background come out from the display and actually help her down to the floor. Mary was a heavyset woman, and this would have been a chore for her by herself. After that, the figure disappeared behind the display and was never seen again. I knew I had a big problem before my first meeting with Mary. When I got the claim, it was about two months old. I was very lucky that the store had kept the tape, because usually they get rid of them within three weeks from the date of the incident.

The adjuster had already contacted Mary, and she had sent him her medical bills and a letter from her attorney in New York stating he was representing her. I started doing a check on the bills and made a few phone calls. I discovered that they were all fake bills. I attempted to contact the attorney in New York, but he did not exist. Later, after Mary was arrested, I discovered that all of the bills that she had sent were simple documents created on her computer, as was the letter from her attorney.

The bills totaled about $10,000. In the insurance game of settling claims, it is normal to double, even triple in some cases, the amount of the medical bills for "pain and suffering." I discovered that Mary had received such compensations on all of the prior claims. I set up a meeting with Mary to interview her, asked if I could videotape, and she agreed. Here are a few of the KDIs (key deception indicators) that Mary exhibited in our interview:

1. She was very loud.

2. Her eye blinks when she was telling her story and answering questions about the fall increased tenfold.

3. When I asked her, "Why should I believe what you just told me?" she answered my question with a question, by asking "Why shouldn't you?"

4. At the same time that she was answering a question with a question, she was laughing for no reason. When Mary asked "Why shouldn't you?" she was displaying uncontrolled laughing by chuckling to herself. I call this a double whammy.

Here is a more detailed overview of the investigation interview I had with Mary.

Mary began by saying that she had stopped at the store to buy diapers for her granddaughter. I asked her about being in the store for twenty minutes and never buying anything, but she did not have an answer for this.

I mentioned in the KDI list Mary's double whammy, but she actually was a triple whammy. The first KDI was the eye blink, the second was the question with a question, and the third was the chuckling at the same time that she answered the question with a question. I have always found that when someone answers my question with a question, they are just stalling because they have to make up a lie. The truth is the truth, and a lie is a lie. Take that to the bank.

In regards to the laughing when she answered the question, it was totally out of place. There was no reason for her to laugh. There was nothing funny about what I was doing and the questions I was asking her, but she laughed.

I took the case to the insurance commissioner's fraud office. They took my investigation, met with the prosecutor, and filed the charges. It went to grand jury, and Mary was arrested. She came into court, pled guilty to the charges of insurance fraud, and got six years in jail.

The truth about her scam finally came out in court. Mary would go to stores and scope out the areas where they had the least amount of camera surveillance. She overlooked the camera that caught her in her alleged fall. She said she would take an empty M&M's plastic tube with her into the store, and it would be filled with baby oil. She would then walk down the aisle and sling it across the floor then lie down in the oil and start screaming. Mary never would give up the name of the person who assisted her in the fall down.

The funny thing about this claim was the fact that I don't think Mary told me the truth about anything that I asked her, except when she gave me her name. She sat there with a straight face and lied and lied, but her body language and her violation of SCAN gave her away, and that was her eventual downfall.

Before my first interview with Mary, I asked her if I could use the recorded interview for training purposes, and she agreed. This still blows my mind. I use the tape of Mary in all of my detection of deception classes. When I interviewed Mary, she displayed so many KDIs, that she was actually off the scale.

"I GOT SOMETHING TO TELL YOU!"

This next case would never have been solved if the insured had not gone into the imminent confession stages before I even suspected he had done anything wrong. We discussed the three stages of imminent confession previously and especially again in chapter 12. I have seen it happen time and time again, especially when I have shown the person that I am interviewing the evidence and they suspect that I am close to discovering their fraud.

I received a claim from an adjuster who had previously taken my *Red Flags* class. I teach this class all over the country, and I teach our adjusters what to look for in fraud claims by giving them a list of red flags that they should look for on a wide variety of claim situations.

The adjuster called and said, "I have a really wealthy guy who has presented a $50,000 burglary, but something is wrong." She said, "You told us if we get a gut feeling that there is a problem, and then there probably is a problem." I told her yes and if she got that feeling, there was probably something wrong. I told her to set up an interview with the insured, myself, and her, and I would see if I got the same feeling when meeting with him. I told her if there was nothing wrong, then we would pay the claim, and she agreed.

We met the insured—I'll call him Edward—at his agent's office. Edward was a successful contractor, approximately mid-forties, and the picture of professionalism and courtesy. He was dressed in a fine suit and wearing the kind of expensive jewelry that demands you take notice of it.

I started this interview the same way I start most of the interviews I conduct: by asking Edward to write down on a piece of paper everything that he did from the time he woke up on the day of the burglary until he went to sleep—classic use of the SCAN technique. When I first took the SCAN course nearly twenty years ago, taught by founder Avinoam Sapir himself, I learned the importance of having the interviewee write down everything that they did on the day of the event and then how to analyze the words that were written.

The interesting thing about Edward is that he got about half-way down the first page, stopped writing, put his pen down on the pad, looked up to the ceiling, let out a sigh, and his chin dropped to his chest. You know the signs of imminent confession by now. Edward had just confessed to something, and I don't even know what he had to confess to. He then picked up his pen and started writing again and finished the paper.

Dying of curiosity as to what he had just confessed to in his writing, I jumped right to the middle of the page where he had stopped and went into confession mode.

In the middle of the page it said this: "then the wife told me how much silverware was taken."

It means a lot in itself when someone says "the wife" instead of "my wife." This means that there is a problem between the two, or it can mean that they are fighting. If the term is used over and over, that marriage is headed for divorce; I can guarantee that.

I still had no clue what he was talking about or why he was ready to confess, but I knew that he was.

He had submitted about thirty pages of items stolen in his initial claim, but I couldn't remember any silverware being on the list.

Trusting in the signs of confession that I knew I had witnessed, I went out on a limb and said to Edward very empathetically, "Is there something you want to tell me about the silverware?"

I could not believe what happened next. He again looked at the ceiling, let out a sigh, his shoulders dropped, and his chin actually went all the way down and touched his chest. I thought, *Here it comes!*

Edward said, "I've got something I need to tell you."

He went on to say that he did have a burglary and his wife told him that all of the silverware was taken, but that was all that was taken. Edward called his agent and told him what happened, and the agent said, "I've got some bad news for you. You had $50,000 worth of silverware taken, but you only have $2,500 in coverage because you didn't schedule the silverware." Edward then told me that he had been told by his wife—or should I say "the wife"—six months ago to get the silverware scheduled, and he failed to do it.

Edward told his agent, "You need to help me out here. The wife will kill me because I didn't schedule the silverware."

The agent told him, "Don't worry about it. We will just fake a loss, and we will just write down $50,000 worth of other items and make up a list."

This is insurance fraud. There is a pretty big difference between $50,000 and $2,500. In an insurance policy, the biggest thing that you can do to get yourself in trouble real quick is through misrepresentation on a claim.

In this case, Edward lied and presented false documents by making up a list of other items stolen that were not stolen and that he never even had. His agent conspired with him on this act.

At this point, Edward's fate was sealed. I told Edward his entire claim would be denied, that I would have to turn the case over to the authorities, and then I asked him to sign an immediate cancellation of his policy, telling him, "Since you have admitted to committing insurance fraud, all coverage with us is hereby cancelled." He signed it without a word.

I then went to the owner of the agency, who wrote Edward's policy, and told him the role that one of his agents had committed in this fraud. He immediately went to the agent's office, fired him, and made him leave the building.

In the end, I reluctantly contacted that state's Department of Insurance, Fraud Division, as required by every state's laws, but they decided not to investigate the case further. Edward was not prosecuted for insurance fraud but definitely had to answer to "the wife" for more than just not scheduling the silverware.

Oftentimes, the person I have discovered to have committed fraud is a good person who got caught up in something they really didn't want to do, felt trapped with limited options, and didn't fully understand the consequences of their actions. Others are in a financial bind, and they have nowhere else to turn; their backs are against the wall financially. Many times when I get a confession or someone walks away from a claim because they know their fraud will surface as a result of my investigation, I honestly tell them, "If I were in your shoes, I could very well have done the same thing that you did. That doesn't make it right, but I do understand why you did what you did." I tell people this with empathy and sympathy and in all sincerity.

THE BOOKIE

This claim takes place in a northern US city. We received a call from our life and health department that they suspected an insured of possibly defrauding them on a health disability policy. I mentioned in an earlier chapter that the one license to steal was to schedule jewelry on an insurance policy. If you remember, anything that happens to it is covered, even if you simply lose it. The second license to steal is a health disability policy. You pay a premium for, let's say, six months. The premium is usually very high, but if you are inured, the policy pays you a set amount per month for the rest of your life. In many cases, once you go on the disability, your premiums are even waived going forward from the date of disability. The insured in this claim—let's call him Gary—had taken out a health disability policy that paid $5,000 per month. He reported that he was injured and had been receiving this monthly payment from us for over two years. The life department got a call from an informant who said that Gary was not injured and the entire claim was a scam. He had supposedly fallen in his driveway and injured his back so badly that he could not continue to work. I was asked to investigate Gary and conduct surveillance to see if he was truly injured.

I solicited two of my associates in SIU to give me a hand on this one, and we also recruited an adjuster in Gary's local area to help us. The first thing we did was check out Gary with a local insurance agent who wrote policies in the area for my company. The agent, a lifelong resident of the area who was very well informed about local illegal activity, advised that he knew Gary to be a high roller, a bookie, and someone who ran numbers for the mob.

Gary lived in a residential neighborhood and drove a high-end sports car that stood out. We tried to follow Gary for two days, but that was a waste of time. He would leave his home and take off, literally, at a hundred miles per hour, and we could never stay with him for very long, even using our four different cars in the effort.

He seemed immune to police arrest, and I later found out that the police in this town were nearly completely controlled by the Mafia, and he was one of the "family."

We did some further checking and discovered that he was a sucker for a good-looking woman. We had such a woman working as an adjuster in this area: Charlene. She was young and very pretty, and we recruited Charlene to help with the investigation.

Our team's goal was to come up with an angle to catch Gary doing something physical that he said he could not due. After putting our heads together, we came up with a plan.

We discovered that our agent in town insured an older man who lived across the street from Gary. This older man did not like Gary, and after we talked with him, he swore our plan to secrecy. He allowed us to set up two video cameras in his garage and use his home as an outpost for our surveillance.

Back when this happened, we were not under many of the same restrictions that we have today regarding what you can do and cannot do on surveillance. This allowed us some leeway in operating that is not available today.

We drove out the night before we started surveillance on Gary and spray painted a yellow line on his curb in front of his house where we wanted Charlene to stop. We asked her to get "all dolled up and looking good" for the next day's work.

Our team watched Gary for three days, recording the schedule that he followed every day. He would usually leave his house about ten o'clock in the morning to make his runs picking up numbers for the mob.

We arrived at the surveillance house across the street from Gary's home about eight o'clock that morning. We set up two video cameras and made sure that each was operating properly. Our host had a perfect setup for this type of surveillance, because he had a garage that faced Gary's home and it had three windows in it. We checked, and if you stood across the street, you could not see inside his garage at all if the lights were not on.

We had another SIU person meet Charlene about two blocks from Gary's home. Just prior to meeting with her, we had taken Charlene's car to a garage and had her lug nuts on one tire tightened with an impact wrench so that they would be extremely hard to remove by hand.

With Charlene just two blocks away from Gary's house, the SIU person let almost all of the air out of her left rear tire. The reason for the left rear tire was so we would have a really good camera view when we were shooting from across the street.

The plan was for Charlene to drive down the street with the flat tire, pull up exactly to our painted spot on the curb, and that spot was where we trained the cameras.

A lot was riding on this. If thirty-year old Gary was faking his injury and we had already paid him $5,000 a month for the last two years and would continue to do so for the rest of his life… millions of dollars were on the line. Gary had no idea we were even looking at him for the fraud, and if we blew this chance and alerted him, we would in all likelihood not get another one.

We specifically told Charlene that she was supposed to pull up to Gary's house, get out, and act extremely frustrated about her car and the flat. The idea was that Gary would see her in front of his house, come outside, change the tire for Charlene, and we would get proof of Gary's lack of disability on tape—case over, busted!

Before she left, we gave Charlene explicit instructions that she was not to enter Gary's home, no matter what, because of Gary's reputation for mistreating women. When Gary came out, she was supposed to tell him that she was very upset with her boss for sending her out in this car with a bad tire, and now she was stranded and didn't know what she would do. Our hope was that Gary's known weakness for attractive ladies would inspire him to help Charlene by exerting himself physically in changing the rigged tire, all while we taped the scene from across the street. Gary's doctors had reported that he could do nothing, that he was almost bedridden because his back was such a mess, and he could perform nearly zero physical activity, much less be expected to work.

Charlene followed instructions perfectly, pulling up exactly to the spot we had painted on the curb in front of Gary's house. She got out and for ten minutes walked around the car, appearing frustrated after opening the trunk only to find no jack (which of course we had removed before she got in the car). At this point, Charlene got nervous that Gary hadn't come outside to help. At this point, things went in a very bad direction. Charlene chose to ignore our warnings and walked up to Gary's door. I looked at my partner and said, "What the heck is she doing?"

Charlene rang the doorbell, and when Gary came to the door, Charlene told him her tire was flat and asked if she could use Gary's phone to call her boss and have someone from work come and change the tire for her.

Charlene then was asked inside by Gary, and our hearts sank as she followed him into the house. We had put this young woman in jeopardy, and we had no communication with her at all. I told my partner that we would give her three minutes; then we would have to blow our cover, run across the street, and probably get into a physical altercation with Gary, a big guy that I sure didn't want to tangle with if I didn't have to.

We were sweating bullets for three solid minutes. Still no Charlene.

My partner and I were just about ready to charge the house when the door suddenly opened and both Gary and Charlene came out laughing and joking around. We let out a sigh of relief— she was okay. Gary came out with a pair of gloves on, and later we were told that when she said she would call her boss he said, "You don't have to do that, baby. I will change the tire for you."

Gary went to the car and looked inside the trunk. Charlene was standing there acting as innocent and helpless as possible, selling her part in this like a professional actor. She was good, real good. After seeing she had no jack, Gary went to his garage and emerged with one. He took out Charlene's spare tire and, just to impress her, lifted it over his head and held it there for a while. Great for the cameras too! Gary then took the tire iron, popped off the hub cap, and attempted to get the lugs off. I don't know if you have ever taken off lug nuts by hand that have been put on with an impact wrench, but it is almost impossible. Gary was learning this fact first hand, but was not to be deterred. He started jumping up and down on the lug spinner over and over. He did things that some healthy men could not physically do, and as a result, our tape was a masterpiece. Gary finally got the tire off after about half an hour of extreme physical exertion, and then, just to again to show his Superman-like capabilities, lifted the flat tire up over his head and put it into the trunk.

Gary then asked Charlene to come back inside the house for a drink. She said thanks but she had an appointment that she was late for already, but would come back later that night.

When Gary started jumping up and down on the lug wrench, my partner and I gave each other a high-five, and we knew that this case was over. Charlene drove away, and Gary went back into his house to wait for his new lady friend who would not be coming back as he had planned.

The surveillance was terminated, and we all met for a lunch celebration.

A week later, after sending Gary a letter stating that our company was discontinuing his disability policy, Gary hired an attorney to handle his case. Gary's attorney contacted us and told him that we would send a tape of his client for him to watch. After Gary's attorney received the tape, they agreed to our cancellation of the disability policy and to pay us back every penny that we had paid Gary over the last two years.

We had developed a plan, our team executed that plan beautifully, and we kept this guy from stealing from us for the rest of his life. I love it when a plan comes together.

CONCLUSION

I hope you have enjoyed this book as much as I have enjoyed writing it. These are all true stories, and I have many of them that I did not have space for in this book. I already have plans for another book if this one is successful. One on the top of my head is the day a drug addict who was an informant thought I was his drug dealer trying to kill him, and he pointed a loaded revolver in my face and was shaking violently with his finger on the trigger, and our insured in that case had a "hit" out on my informant. You will love that one.

For those of you that have been in my classes I teach, this book is for you. If you had not said to me over and over again that I should write it, it would have never happened.

I love my job and have for thirty-four years now. I will continue to fight fraud as long as my health allows me. The main reason I continue to do it is this is what I was meant to do, and I think I am pretty good at it. Thanks for reading, and have a great life.

CPSIA information can be obtained at www.ICGtesting.com
Printed in the USA
LVOW08s1755090315

429814LV00001B/141/P